CNC Router Essentials

Text © 2018, 2020 by Randy Johnson

Photographs © 2018, 2020 by Randy Johnson, unless otherwise noted
Photographs on front cover and pages 8; 40, bottom; 132, middle; 133, top left; 134, all; 135, all; 136,
right middle and bottom; 138, all; 139, all, courtesy Next Wave Automation
Photographs on page 48, top; 132, bottom; 133, top right and bottom; 136, left and top right; 137, all,
courtesy ShopBot Tools, Inc.
Photograph on page 132, top, courtesy Axiom
Photographs on pages 60, 76, 92, and 108 © 2018 by Danielle Atkins

Publisher: Paul McGahren
Copy Editor: Kerri Grzybicki
Designer: Lindsay Hess
Layout Designer: Jodie Delohery
Indexer: Jay Kreider

Cedar Lane Press
PO Box 5424
Lancaster, PA 17606-5424

ISBN: 978-1-950934-12-6

Library of Congress Control Number: 2020930297

Printed in the United States of America

10 9 8 7 6 5 4 3 2 1

Note: The following list contains names used in **CNC Router Essentials** that may be registered with the United
States Copyright Office: Adobe Illustrator; Aspire; Axiom; Fusion 360; Harrington; Instagram; Next Wave
Automation; Onshape; Pinterest; Rhino; ShopBot Tools, Inc.; SketchUp; VCarve Pro; Vectric.

The information in this book is given in good faith; however, no warranty is given, nor are results guaranteed.
Woodworking is inherently dangerous. Your safety is your responsibility. Neither Cedar Lane Press nor the
author assume any responsibility for any injuries or accidents.

To learn more about Cedar Lane Press books, or to find a retailer near you,
email info@cedarlanepress.com or visit us at www.cedarlanepress.com.

CNC Router Essentials

Basics for Mastering the Most Innovative Tool in Your Workshop

Randy Johnson

CEDAR LANE PRESS

Contents

CHAPTER

1

CNC Basics

Let's start your CNC journey by helping you understand a few key aspects of working with a CNC machine:

- **CNC machine mechanics**
- **CNC workflow**
- **CNC software**

Machine mechanics

Basic CNC (computer numerical controlled) routers operate on three axes: X, Y, and Z, **Image 1.1**. Think back to your days of graphing in math class. The X and Y axes move left to right and front to back, while the Z axis is vertical. The machine can move in all three directions at one time, which allows it to cut complex shapes as easily as simple shapes. Most CNC routers use an industrial high-speed spindle, although some CNCs use woodworking-style router motors to hold the bit or cutting tool, **Images 1.2**. The main differences are spindles run quieter and are more accurate than woodworking routers, plus a spindle's bearings last several times longer than those in a woodworking router,

but a spindle costs several times the price of a similarly sized router. Some CNC tools allow you to start with a router motor and later upgrade to a spindle. The bed or deck of a CNC machine may be metal, plastic, or plywood, and is often covered with a spoilboard, **Image 1.3**. The spoilboard is usually a sheet of MDF or plywood. It is a consumable item, since many projects require you to cut completely through the project material and slightly into the spoilboard. Over time the spoilboard will become grooved, but you can renew it by routing the surface flat. When the spoilboard becomes too thin, it can be replaced, or a new one can be glued on top of the old one.

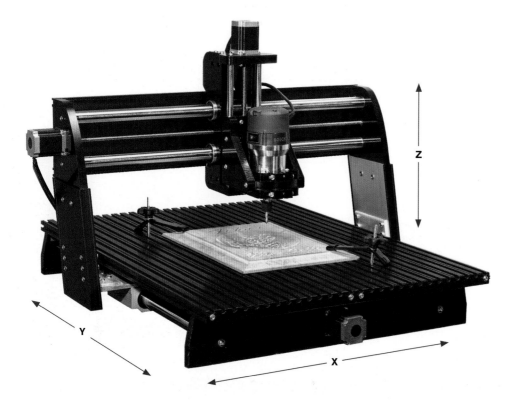

Image 1.1: Three-axis CNC machines move in three directions. The Z axis controls vertical movement. The X and Y axes control the left to right, and front to back movement. The X and Y are reversed on some machines.

Images 1.2: An industrial spindle (left) or woodworking router (right) is used to hold the router bit on a CNC machine. Spindles run quieter than routers and last longer, but cost several times more. Spindles are available as either fan-cooled or water-cooled. Water-cooled spindles are often less expensive, but water-cooled spindles require a reservoir and pump to circulate the water.

Image 1.3: A spoilboard usually covers the machine bed to protect it during cutting, since many CNC operations involve cutting slightly through the project material. The spoilboard is considered a consumable and replaceable part of the machine.

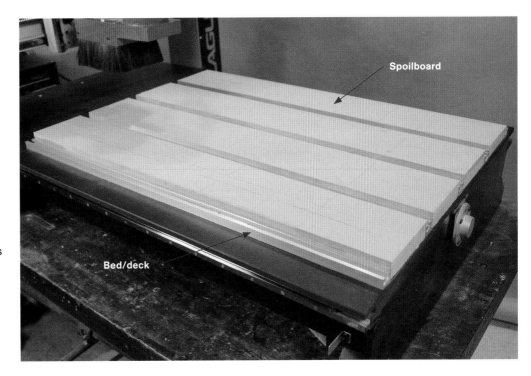

The brain of a CNC consists of onboard electronics connected to an external computer or control pendant, **Images 1.4**. Together these are referred to as the control system. The control system automatically moves the machine during operation, but can also be used by the operator to manually move the spindle along the machine axes during tool setup.

CNC workflow

The workflow for CNC projects consists of three primary steps: designing, toolpathing, and machining, **Image 1.5**. Each of these has several sub-steps that we'll discuss in later chapters, but the important thing to know is that they are each associated with a particular kind of software. CAD (computer-aided drawing) for drawing; CAM (computer-aided machining), which converts the CAD drawing to toolpaths and machine code; and the Controller software that communicates the code to the CNC machine and tells it where to move during the machining process. Don't let that alphabet soup of letters intimidate you. Using today's CNC machines has been simplified by advances in CNC software that automates much of the complex processes of the past. With a little practice, it will start to make sense, but first, let's take a quick look at each type of software.

Images 1.4: CNC machines connect to either a control computer or a control pendant. These allow the operator to control the movements of the CNC machine automatically and manually.

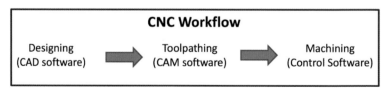

Image 1.5: A specific type of software is associated with each step of the CNC workflow.

CNC software

There are dozens of CAD programs that can be used to create CNC project designs. So, if you currently use a CAD program that you like, you can probably use it as a starting point. The basic requirement is that it needs to output a CAM compatible file such as a .dxf, .dwg, .skp, .eps, .ai, or similar vector-based file. A software package that is compatible with many types of CNC machines is called VCarve Pro by Vectric. It's popular because it combines both CAD (designing) and CAM (toolpathing) software in one package. It was also developed specifically as a CNC application. It's also one of the easiest to learn. We use VCarve Pro v8.5 for the illustrations in this book. If you use a different version, your CAD/CAM tools may vary from what shown. You can download a free demo copy at Vectric.com. If you use a different CAD or CAM software, the steps will be similar.

VCarve Pro has three main windows, **Image 1.6**. The CAD side is used to create lines, shapes, and text. It also contains tools for aligning and refining the elements in your design. The center workspace is used to create, edit, and view your designs and toolpaths in both 2-D and 3-D. The CAM

Image 1.6: CAD software is used to create shapes, add text, and edit project designs. CAM tools convert the design into toolpaths. VCarve Pro software (shown here) conveniently includes both CAD and CAM in one software package.

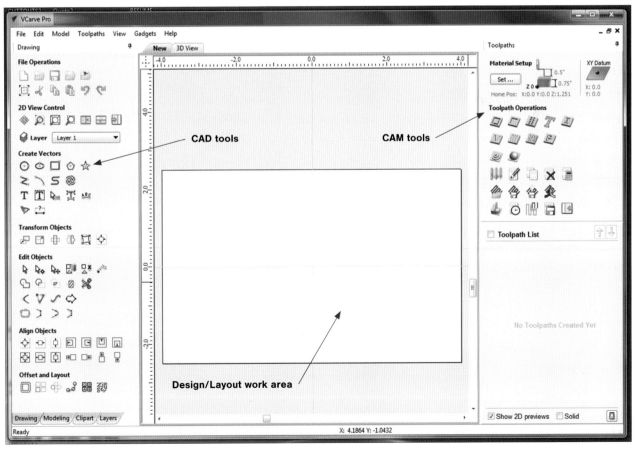

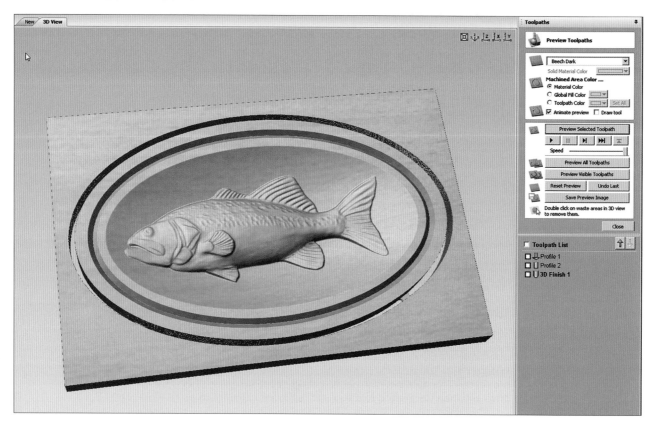

Image 1.7: One of the most helpful features of VCarve Pro is its ability generate a toolpath preview. The 3-D representation of your project will help you refine your design and find toolpath errors.

side is used to create the toolpaths for your project. Creating toolpaths involves setting parameters, including the kind of bit, the type of cut, the depth of cut, the number of passes, and the feeds and speeds for the bit.

One of the best parts of VCarve Pro is that after the toolpath is created, you can preview the virtual results, **Image 1.7**. It's a great way to proof your work, catch errors, and verify that your project looks correct before cutting. If everything looks good, you can save your toolpath through a process called post-processing (also part of VCarve Pro), which converts your toolpaths to machine code. Post processors are machine specific, so be sure you choose the correct one for your CNC. This cutting file

is then saved and loaded directly into the control software from your computer or via flash drive to the computer or pendant that is attached to the CNC machine, **Image 1.8**.

Control software usually comes with the CNC machine because it needs to be configured to match the machine's mechanical and electrical setup, **Image 1.9**. Some machines use a pendant to control the machine, while others are hooked directly to a computer. Both contain similar functions for controlling the machine, because their primary function is to aid the operator in preparing the machine for cutting, and then reading the cutting file and directing the CNC's movements.

Images 1.8: Toolpaths are converted to machine code using a post processor. This step creates a cutting file that is usually saved to a flash drive and then transferred to the control software at the machine.

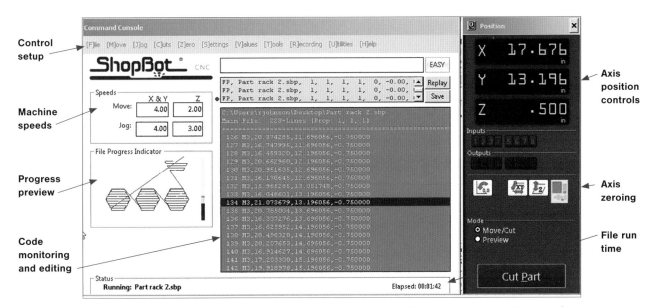

Image 1.9: CNC machine control software is often brand specific, but they all contain many of the same options for controlling and monitoring the machine. Control pendants also have many of these control options built into them.

CHAPTER

2

Design Essentials

CNC project designs fall into two general types: 2-D line drawings and 3-D models. They can be created in a variety of ways and even combined. In this chapter, we'll look at:

- **Basic design types**
- **The basics of creating and using 2-D line drawing**
- **The basics of creating and using 3-D models**
- **Sources of project inspiration**

Using 2-D designs

A wide variety of CNC work can be accomplished using just 2-D lines, **Image 2.1.** Any CAD program can be used to create a 2-D line design, but designs must be saved as or converted to a vector line format to be compatible with the CAM toolpathing software. A vector line is made up of points that represent the geometry of the line, **Image 2.2.** One big benefit of a vector line design is that you can scale it up or down without losing details or resolution. Most CAD programs can create vector line designs, **Image 2.3.** Common vector file formats include .dxf, .esp, .dwg, .ai, and some .pdf files. These various file formats

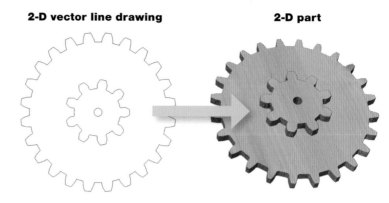

2-D vector line drawing   **2-D part**

Image 2.1: A 2-D line design creates a part that looks like it has been cut out on a bandsaw.

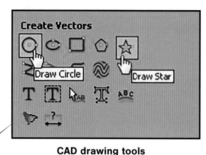

CAD drawing tools

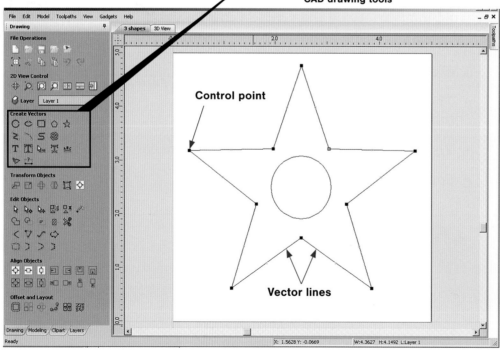

Image 2.2: The basis of all 2-D CNC design work is the creation of vector lines. Vector lines are made up of control points, and can be scaled larger or smaller without losing any detail. CAM programs use vector lines to create the toolpath cutting files. VCarve Pro (shown here) contains CAD drawing tools that create vector lines by default.

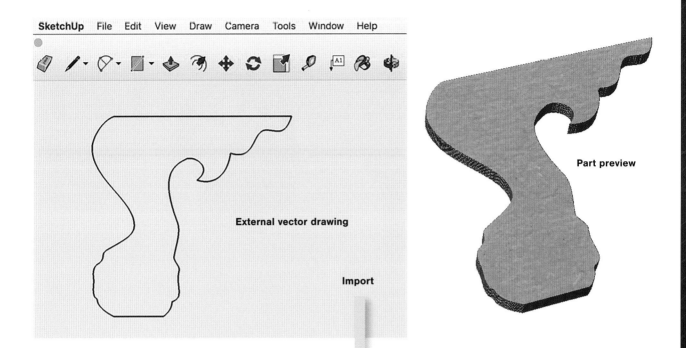

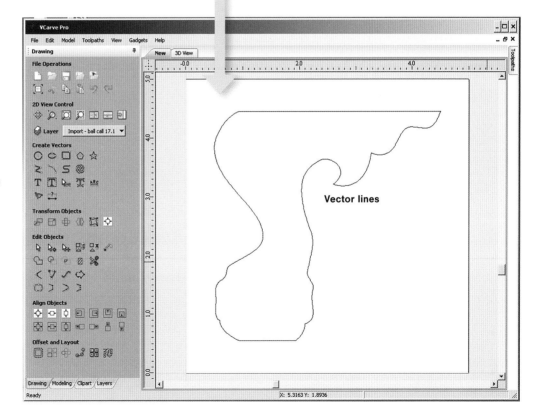

Image 2.3: Most CAD programs are capable of creating the vector lines, which can easily be imported into a CAM program for toolpath creation. So, if you are currently using a CAD program that creates or exports vector line drawing (e.g., .dxf, .eps, .dwg) you can probably keep using it as your primary CAD design tool.

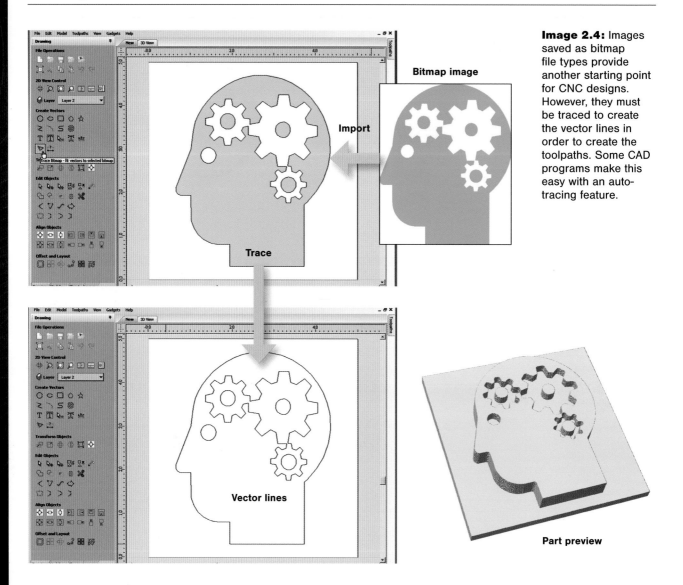

Image 2.4: Images saved as bitmap file types provide another starting point for CNC designs. However, they must be traced to create the vector lines in order to create the toolpaths. Some CAD programs make this easy with an auto-tracing feature.

are also easily read by most CAD programs. Predesigned vector art is also readily available online—some for purchase and some for free. It's an excellent way to find high-quality designs for CNC projects.

Bitmap images such as colored clipart and high contrast photos provide another starting point for 2-D designs, **Image 2.4**. Some of the common bitmap file types are .bmp, .jpg, .gif, .tif, and .png. Unlike

vector designs, bitmaps cannot be read by CAM software and need to be traced to create useable vector lines. Some CAD software packages (including VCarve Pro) provide a built-in bitmap to vector line tracing tool. You can even start with a hand sketch. Simply photograph it and import it for tracing. It's a powerful way to create original hand-drawn CNC project designs.

Using 3-D models

CNCs excel in their ability to cut complex shapes, and this includes 3-D models, **Image 2.5.** There are some limits, but the first thing to understand is that 3-D models fit into one of three groups. The first is

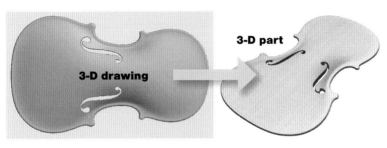

Image 2.5: A 3-D model creates a part that appears sculpted or carved.

a single-sided model, such a carved door panel or sign. The second type is a two-sided shape, such as coin or fish. The third type is a full in-the-round shape, such as a coffee mug, human figure, or automobile. Each type becomes progressively more challenging to carve on the CNC. Single- and two-sided CNC 3-D carving are the most straightforward, and these are covered in the practice project chapters. Full in-the-round models, such as a car, can sometimes be carved using a multi-sided carving setup on a 3-axis CNC, but other 3-D models require a 5-axis CNC machine and advanced CAM software.

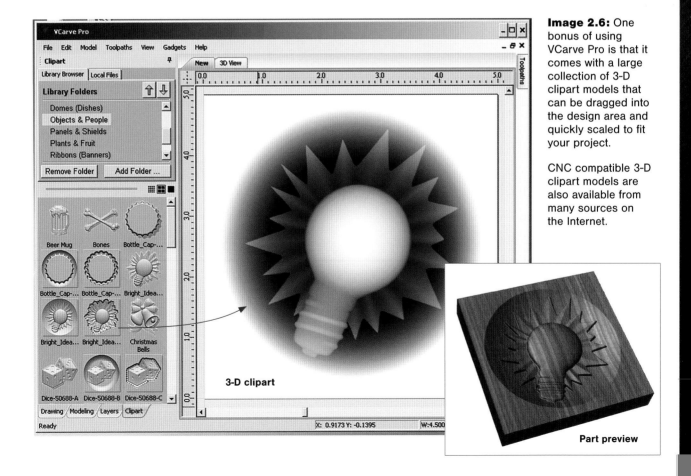

Image 2.6: One bonus of using VCarve Pro is that it comes with a large collection of 3-D clipart models that can be dragged into the design area and quickly scaled to fit your project.

CNC compatible 3-D clipart models are also available from many sources on the Internet.

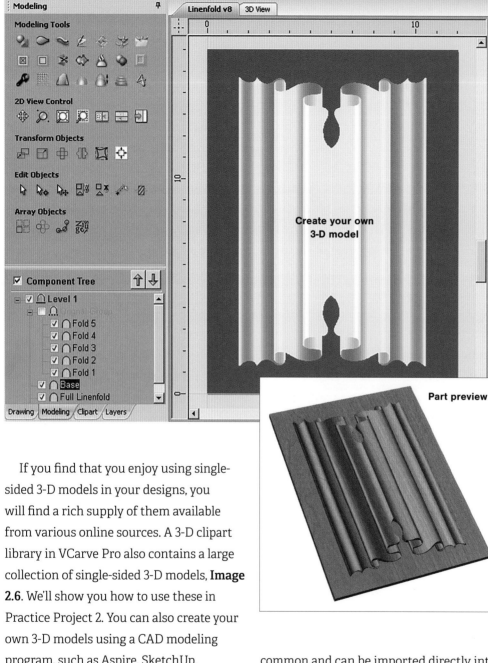

Image 2.7: Creating 3-D models can be accomplished with any one of several CAD modeling programs. Aspire (shown here) has a dedicated menu of 3-D modeling tools for creating single-sided models, such as the linen fold door. Creating a 3-D model takes time and skill, but fortunately, there are lots of CNC-compatible 3-D models available on the Internet that you can import into VCarve Pro, Aspire, or other CAD/CAM programs.

If you find that you enjoy using single-sided 3-D models in your designs, you will find a rich supply of them available from various online sources. A 3-D clipart library in VCarve Pro also contains a large collection of single-sided 3-D models, **Image 2.6**. We'll show you how to use these in Practice Project 2. You can also create your own 3-D models using a CAD modeling program, such as Aspire, SketchUp, Fusion 360, Rhino, Onshape, and others, **Image 2.7**. Once you've created a 3-D model, you need to save it in a CAM-compatible file format. The .stl file type is one of the most common and can be imported directly into CAD/CAM programs, such as VCarve Pro, to create the 3-D carving toolpaths. Be aware though, that .stl files, like bitmap images, lose resolution when they are scaled up in size because an .stl shape is a wire mesh. As you scale up the model, the mesh becomes visible as flat triangular facets, which will also be visible in the final carving. The best defense against this is to use a high-resolution .stl designed for CNC design work and preview the .stl in the CAD/CAM software before committing it to your design.

Project inspiration

Where can you find project ideas? Well, a simple web search or a visit to Pinterest or Instagram will reveal thousands of pictures of CNC work. A little more searching will reveal sites with ready-to-machine CNC project plans—some for sale and some for free. After you get some experience, lots of existing DIY shop projects (wood, plastic, aluminum) can be converted to CNC projects. It's a great idea to network with other CNC owners: join a forum or a user group. Some of these groups hold meetings with show-and-tell time, providing a close-up look at completed CNC projects and the opportunity to ask questions about how the person made them.

Signs

Making signs is an immensely popular application of CNC machines and an excellent way to gain some experience at CNC project design and machining. Plus, existing signs are all around and can be a rich source of inspiration. You will learn a lot about sign design by just looking at existing signs in your neighborhood. Even if the sign wasn't CNC cut, study its layout and shape and then use those elements in your designs. If you see something you like, whether it's painted, hand carved, laser engraved, or molded, grab the idea and archive it.

Think outside the box

As you look for ideas, don't discount anything as a possibility. When you're new to CNC, it's easy to look at something and think it's too hard. But as your skills increase, you'll want to have more challenging projects. If you like it, capture it, and then figure out later how to execute it.

Keep your ideas organized

With today's smartphones and tablets, and the fluid nature of the Internet, it's easy to grab ideas no matter where you are. Maybe too easy, since it makes keeping all these files organized a challenge. There are many approaches to this with today's technology. At a minimum, keep your ideas organized by category so you can find them as your collection grows deeper and deeper.

From inception to completion, you can let your creative juices flow with CNC work. Keep in mind that, in addition to wood, CNC machines can cut aluminum, brass, bronze, foam, and a variety of other materials. Start stockpiling those ideas!

CHAPTER

CHAPTER 3

Toolpath Essentials

Once you draw a project in CAD, you then create toolpaths to cut the project. Setting up a toolpath requires a number of steps, but none are difficult or involve writing code. Plan to practice the steps virtually in software a few times before making test cuts on your machine. In this chapter, you'll learn about:

- **Router bits for CNC**
- **Four frequently used toolpaths**
- **The importance of chip load**
- **Determining the best feeds and speeds**
- **The primary steps in setting up a toolpath**

Router bits

Many of the bits you use with your handheld router or router table can be used in your CNC. There are also specialized bits for CNC that you will find useful. Carbide-tipped or solid carbide bits are the most commonly used bits on CNC routers because they stand up to abrasive materials such as MDF and plywood. However, due to their hardness, they are also more susceptible to breakage than high-speed steel (HSS). HSS also has the advantage of being less expensive than carbide, although HSS bits generally dull quicker.

You probably already own a few straight bits. These are good general purpose bits, but won't give you the cut quality of a spiral bit. Spiral bits are available as upcut, downcut, or a combination, **Image 3.1**. Upcut bits act like a drill bit, pulling chips up out of the cut, which keeps the cutting path clear. The spiral creates a shearing action that reduces chipping and gives you a better edge quality on your material than a straight fluted bit. An upcut bit may fray or chip the top surface of your material, but when through cutting, it provides a chip-free cut on the bottom side.

Downcut spiral bits push down toward the material. This downward shear action provides chip-free cutting on the top surface but may cause chipping on the bottom of some materials, such as melamine and plywood. Downcut spiral bits are also useful when cutting thin materials because the downcut pressure helps to hold the material against the bed

A router bit starter set

- 60 and 90° V-bits (V-carving)
- ¼"-, ⅜"-, and ½"-diameter upcut spiral straight bits (general cutting)
- ⅛" ballnose bit (3-D finish carving)

rather than lifting it, which can occur with an upcut bit. Because a downcut bit pushes the chips down when cutting, the chips usually get packed into the kerf. The packed-in chips will fall away when you separate the finished parts. If you need to remove them before that, try running the cut a second time to loosen up the chips and then remove them with compressed air or a vacuum.

Compression bits combine upcut and downcut shearing action in one bit and thus leave a clean cut on both the top and bottom side of your material.

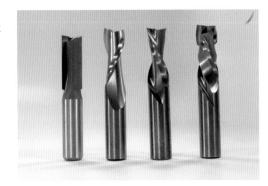

Image 3.1: Straight bits come in a variety of configurations. The four shown here are (left to right): straight flute, upcut spiral end mill, downcut spiral end mill, and compression end mill.

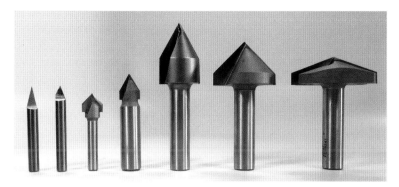

Image 3.2: V-bits are available in different diameters and angles. They are mostly used for V-carving.

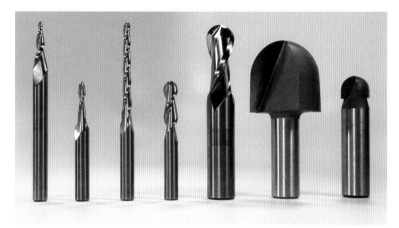

Image 3.3: Ballnose and core box bits are available in a variety of diameters and lengths. Smaller diameters are tapered to increase strength and reduce breakage. Spiral ballnose bits are commonly used to machine intricate 3-D carving designs. For shallow low-detail carvings, a core box bit works well. Both bits can be used to create fluted designs.

Image 3.4: A large diameter spoilboard bit is used to surface the MDF table when it becomes rough.

Additional useful bits

As you do more with your machine you may want to add:

- 30° V-bit (fine V-carving and details)
- ¹⁄₁₆"- and ¼"-diameter ballnose bits (3-D carving)
- ¼"-diameter downcut spiral straight bit (general cutting)
- ⅛"-diameter straight bit (fine profile and pocket cuts)

V-bits are most commonly used for V-carving text and other fine details, **Image 3.2**. The smaller the angle of the V-bit, the finer the details it will be able to cut.

Ballnose and core box bits are available in a variety of diameters and lengths, **Image 3.3**. Tapered ballnose bits are used for finishing intricate 3-D carvings. Like V-bits, smaller bits will create more intricate details.

A spoilboard or fly cutter bit is helpful, but not imperative when starting out, **Image 3.4**. This type of bit is used to level the spoilboard on your machine. With its large diameter, it can cover a big area quickly. You can also surface your spoilboard with something more common, such as a ¾" straight bit. It just takes longer.

Which bits you'll need for your work depends largely on the types of projects you plan to make, but here is a short list of bits that will get you started, and you can add to it as your needs expand.

Frequently used toolpaths

A CNC machine can make many types of cuts, but the four most commonly used are the Profile, Pocket, V-Carve, and 3-D Roughing and Finishing Toolpaths, **Image 3.5**. With an understanding and mastery of these cuts, you'll be able to complete a variety of projects.

Pocket cuts are used to create a recessed area in your workpiece, **Image 3.6**. The recess might simply be a design detail in your project, or it can be sized to accept another piece of material, such as butterfly inlay. A pocket cut can be square, rectangular, oval, or nearly any shape you can imagine.

V-carving is used to create text that simulates incised handcarved lettering, **Image 3.7**. But it works equally well on any "closed" line shape, such as the outline of an animal. By contrast, a single line with ends that don't connect is considered an "open" line shape and cannot be V-carved. V-Carve is a very popular toolpath with CNC users and is a very simple way to add decorative carving to your project.

3-D carving toolpaths include both roughing and finishing passes. They are used to carve 3-D models. The roughing pass is used to quickly remove the excess material and usually done with a straight bit, **Image 3.8**. The finishing pass is almost always done with a ballnose bit to create the fine details, **Image 3.9**. The diameters of the roughing and finishing bits depend on the size and detail of your project.

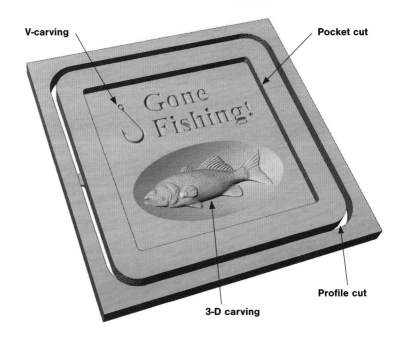

Image 3.5: A CNC can make many types of cuts, but these four are the most commonly used ones. In the world of CNC, these cuts are also referred to as toolpaths.

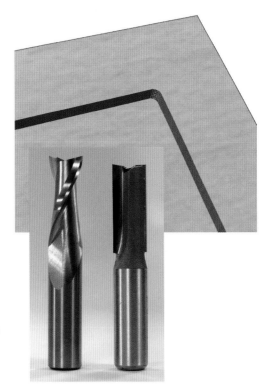

Image 3.6: The *Pocket Toolpath* typically uses a straight bit of some type to cut the recessed area.

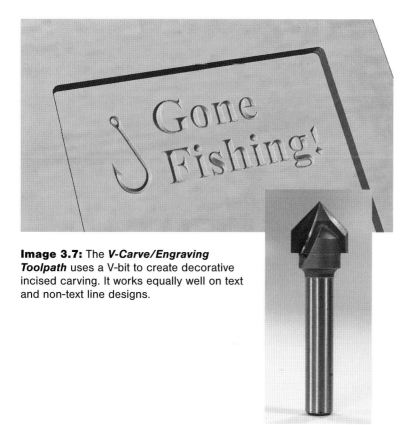

Image 3.7: The *V-Carve/Engraving Toolpath* uses a V-bit to create decorative incised carving. It works equally well on text and non-text line designs.

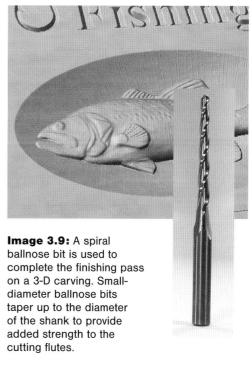

Image 3.9: A spiral ballnose bit is used to complete the finishing pass on a 3-D carving. Small-diameter ballnose bits taper up to the diameter of the shank to provide added strength to the cutting flutes.

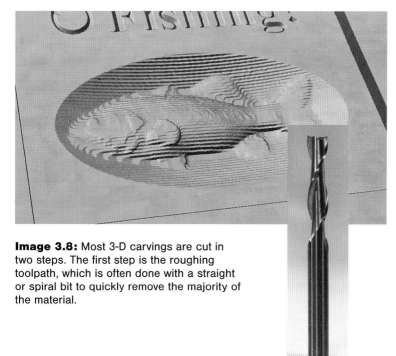

Image 3.8: Most 3-D carvings are cut in two steps. The first step is the roughing toolpath, which is often done with a straight or spiral bit to quickly remove the majority of the material.

Profile cuts can be used to cut partly or completely through your work, **Image 3.10**. Think of it as a saw blade or dado blade that makes a cut partially or completely through the material. It is commonly used to separate the part from the surrounding material or to create grooves and slots.

With these four types of CNC cuts, you can create a variety unique projects. Yet, we've only scratched the surface of what can be done with these cuts, as there are many other ways they can be used to enhance your CNC projects.

Cutting direction

Climb cutting with a handheld router or router table (moving in the same direction the router bit is spinning) can be dangerous since the bit can grab the material and cause you to lose control of the tool. With a CNC, this is not a concern, **Image 3.11,** and you can reap the primary benefit of climb cutting, which is that it reduces grain chipping when cutting solid wood. Conventional cutting is commonly used for other materials or as a finishing pass after climb cutting. Sometimes determining the best cutting direction requires running a test cut and then examining both sides of the cut and choosing the one with the best edge quality. Whichever cutting direction you use, the goal is a smooth edge that's best for your project. On projects with exposed edges, you can expect to do about the same amount of sanding as you would when using a handheld router or router table.

Offset and raster

Achieving a smooth surface at the bottom of a pocket cut can be a challenge. First, make sure you are using a bit designed for bottom cutting in your material. Generally, this will be some a type of end mill bit. Then give some thought to the pocket clearing direction for the cut. Two common ones include offset and raster, **Image 3.12**. Think of offset cutting as a spiral motion, and raster as a straight-line motion. Raster can be set up to cut in the X or Y direction or at an angle. Think about machining a piece of wood. You typically get the best cut quality by going with the grain, or at an angle. So, when you're concerned about the quality of the finished cut, setting the raster cut parallel to the

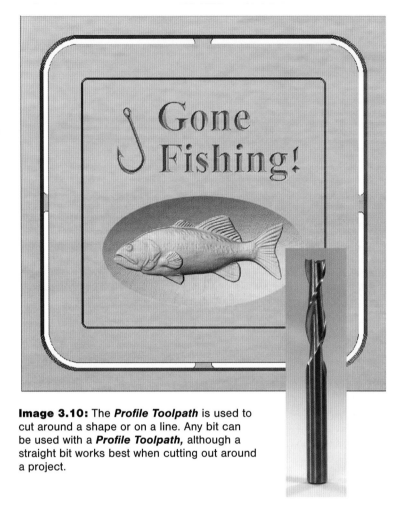

Image 3.10: The *Profile Toolpath* is used to cut around a shape or on a line. Any bit can be used with a *Profile Toolpath,* although a straight bit works best when cutting out around a project.

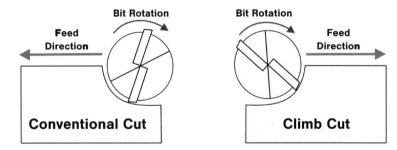

Image 3.11: As a general practice, use climb cutting for solid wood and conventional cutting for other materials, but run some tests to determine which feed direction produces the best edge quality for your particular material and bit. Sometimes a combination of the two feed directions is used to produce the desired results.

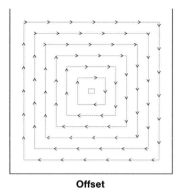
Offset

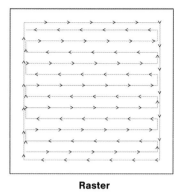
Raster

Image 3.12: There are two basic ways to clear a pocket. Offset clearing is slightly quicker than raster clearing, but raster clearing with the grain on wood projects leaves fewer noticeable tool marks.

CHIP LOADS FOR STRAIGHT BITS				
Material	**⅛" dia.**	**¼" dia.**	**⅜" dia.**	**½" dia.**
Hardwood	.003 –.005	.009 –.011	.015 –.018	.019 –.021
Softwood	.004 –.006	.011 –.013	.017 –.020	.021 –.023
Plywood	.004 –.007	.011 –.013	.017 –.020	.021 –.023
MDF	.004 –.007	.013 –.016	.020 –.023	.025 –.027
Hard Plastic	.002 –.004	.006 –.009	.008 –.010	.010 –.012
Soft Plastic	.003 –.006	.007 –.010	.010 –.012	.010 –.012
Aluminum	.002 –.005	.003 –.0 06	.004 –.008	.010 –.012

Image 3.13: Chip loads change with the hardness of the material and the diameter of the bit. The horsepower of the spindle or router is also a factor, so running a test cut is always a good idea. Once you find a bit and speed combination that works well for a particular material, record the information for future use.

Setting feeds and speeds

A CNC machine does work that is very similar to what you may already be doing with a handheld router or router table. When you use these handheld power tools, you get constant tactile feedback about the cutting action. In response, you make adjustments as you go, decreasing the feed rate of the tool or material when you hear the router bogging down, or increasing the feed speed if you smell the wood getting hot or burning. We don't get this tactile feedback from a CNC machine, but the concerns are the same. While it's possible to change some CNC settings while the machine is operating, it's not commonly done for regular cutting. Rather the feeds and speeds are programmed into the toolpath. This topic of setting feeds and speeds is one of the most confusing aspects of learning to operate a CNC. But like many things, once you understand the basics, it becomes a little like riding a bike.

The easiest way to determine the best feed and speed rates for your project is to start with the recommended chip load number for your material and bit. Most major bit manufacturers publish chip load numbers for their bits and various materials. If you can't locate those numbers, use the chip load chart provided in this chapter, **Image 3.13**. It works with most straight bits. Once you have the recommended chip load number for your material, enter it along with the bit information into a chip load calculator to determine the recommended speed or feed

grain direction will usually give you the best cut quality. As you gain experience, you'll learn what works best with your material and router bit combination, and of course, run some tests to determine the best settings.

The importance of chip load

Simply put, chip load is the thickness of the chip that the router bit removes during cutting, **Image 3.14**. Different types of materials have different recommended chip loads, usually in given as a range to accommodate variations in material hardness and machines. Achieving a good chip load has two benefits. One, it helps keep the bit cool, which significantly increases bit life. Second, it saves time because you're not spinning your wheels creating dust. Using the right chip load allows your bit to cut more effectively and efficiently. Chip load is affected by your machine's X, Y, Z feed rates, the RPM speed of the bit, and the number of flutes on the bit, **Image 3.15**. Changing any of these will affect the chip load. Feeding too fast may burden your machine, or create chatter or mill marks on the edge of your material. Feeding too slow or using too high of spindle speed will create dust and possibly burn or burnish the edge of your material— none of these are useful outcomes.

Image 3.14: Using the correct feed and speed settings will produce chips when routing, even in dust-prone materials such as MDF. Producing chips is important because they carry the heat away from the bit, which increases the life of the cutting edge.

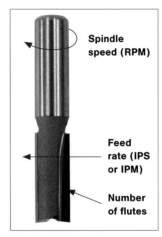

Spindle speed (RPM)

Feed rate (IPS or IPM)

Number of flutes

Image 3.15: The three variables that control chip thickness (chip load) are spindle speed, feed rate, and the number of flutes.

rate, **Image 3.16**. Most CNC control software packages include a chip load calculator, but there are also many available for free on the Internet. Or if you want to do it longhand, here's the math:

Feed Rate (inch per **minute**) / (RPM x number of flutes) = **Chip Load**

Feed Rate (inches per **second** x 60) / (RPM x number of flutes) = **Chip Load**

The depth you cut with each cutting pass does not affect the chip load, but it is an important consideration because cutting too aggressively can cause the bit to break, as well as slow or stall the machine. Here are some recommended pass depths for a range of bits and machines:

- Light-duty CNC machines, and bits under ¼" dia. (about half of the bit diameter or less)
- Small- and medium-duty CNC machines (1 time the diameter or less)
- Full-size and heavy-duty CNC machines (1 to 2 times the diameter and greater)

Image 3.16: Using a chip load calculator is the simplest way to determine CNC feeds and speeds. Many CNC tools have a chip load calculator included with their control software, and there are many calculators available on the Internet. Or you can calculate the chip load using one of the formulas.

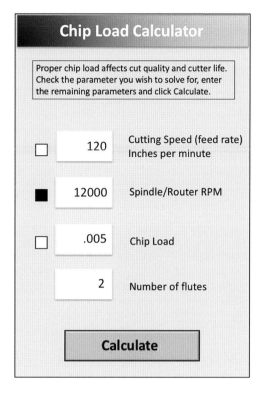

It's always valuable to run a few test cuts to verify that your chip load settings produce the desired results. When test cutting, check for these three things:

1. You're making chips, not dust.
2. The edge quality is good.
3. Your CNC machine isn't bogging down.

To increase chip load (make bigger chips) do one or a combination of the following:

- Decrease the RPM.
- Increase feed rate.
- Use a bit with fewer flutes.

To decrease chip load (make smaller chips) do one or a combination of the following:

- Increase the RPM.
- Decrease the feed rate.
- Use a bit with more flutes.

If the chip load seems correct, but your machine is bogging down, try decreasing the depth of cut and/or the amount of bit stepover.

The Tool Database

Once you've determined the correct feeds and speeds for your bit and material, enter the information into the Tool Database of the CAM software, **Image 3.17**. That way you can use it again the next time you cut a similar project. The Tool Database in VCarve Pro is customizable so that you can add and delete bits as your bit collection grows and changes. You can even create multiple copies of the same bit—each with its own set of parameters. This is useful when you want to set up one bit for different applications. For example, you may have a ¼" end mill bit that you use for both softwood and hardwood, but each application uses a different set of feeds and speeds.

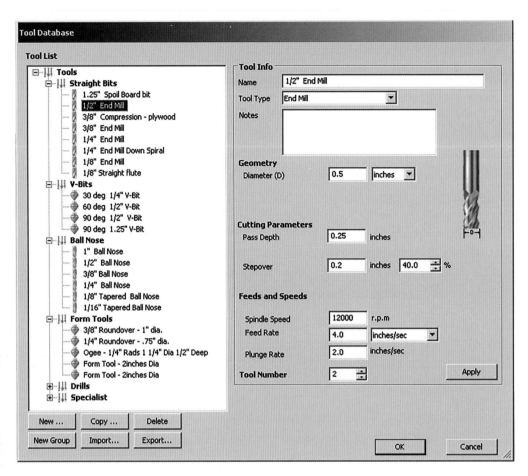

Tool Database in the CAM software is used to store the cutting parameters for bits and other types of cutting tools. The lists are editable so you can add and delete information to match your bit collection.

One important thing to be aware of is that the RPM settings in the Tool Database are not read by CNC machines that lack automatic speed control. For these machines, you need to manually adjust the router/spindle speed at the machine before you run the toolpath. How this is done varies between machines, but your owner's manual should provide the information. Most larger CNC machines can receive this RPM information and will automatically adjust the speed accordingly, which is very convenient.

Creating a toolpath

There's a lot to consider when setting up a toolpath, but the five basic steps are:

1. Select the vector lines
2. Set the cutting depth
3. Select and set up up the bit
4. Set remaining parameters
5. Preview and save the toolpath

These five steps are described in more detail in the following pages of this chapters.

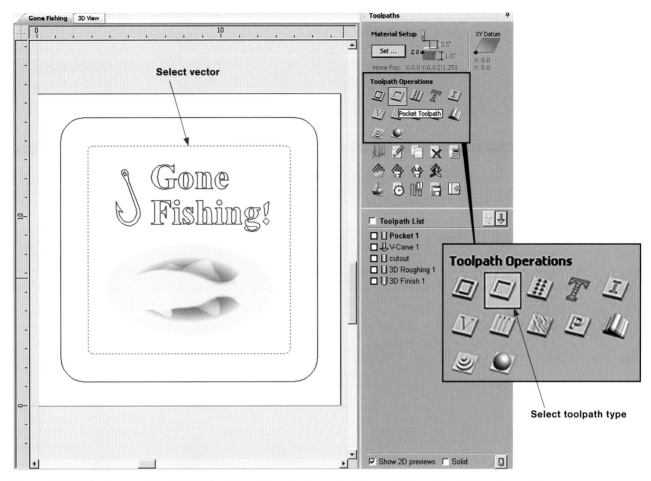

Image 3.18: Creating a toolpath: the first step is to select a vector line or 3-D model and then choose the appropriate toolpath.

Step 1: Select the line vectors

Begin by selecting the line vector(s) or model. Then select the toolpath type. In this example, we'll use the Pocket Toolpath to cut out the center of the sign, **Image 3.18**.

In the world of CAM software, there are many types of toolpaths. The main ones that come with VCarve Pro include Profile, Pocket, Drilling, Quick Engrave, Inset, V-Carve, Fluting, Texture, Prism Carving, Molding, 3-D Roughing, and 3-D Finishing.

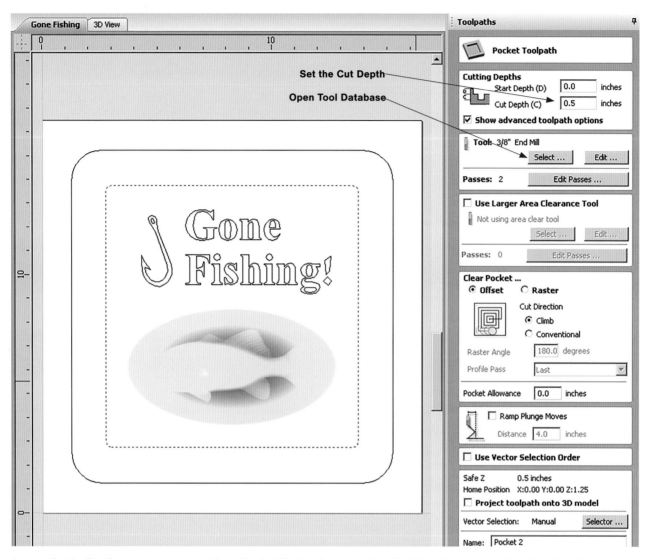

Image 3.19: The first parameter to set for a *Pocket Toolpath* is to set the *Cut Depth,* then open the *Tool Database* (library) and select the bit for your project.

Step 2: Set the Cut Depth

In the Pocket Toolpath window, set the Cut Depth, **Image 3.19**. Then open the Tool Database by clicking on the Select button in the Tools menu.

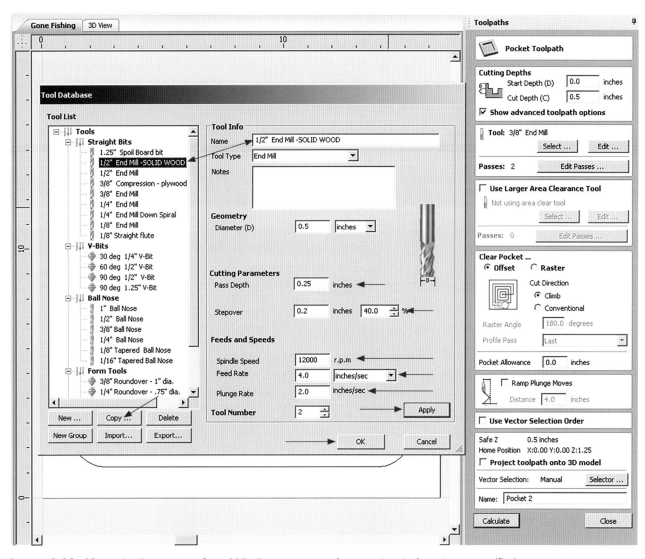

Image 3.20: After selecting your preferred bit, there are several parameters to be set up or verified.

Step 3: Choose and set up the bit

The Tool Database has a list of available bits, **Image 3.20**. Choose the appropriate bit for your project—in this case, the ½" end mill for solid wood. Then set the following:

    a. Pass Depth

    b. Stepover

    c. Spindle Speed

    d. Feed Rate

    e. Plunge Rate

You can Copy a tool and save it with its unique settings and name (e.g., ½" End Mill - SOLID WOOD). You can have multiple copies of the same bit, each with its own unique name and set of parameters. Setting up a bit with its material-specific parameters saves you time the next time you run the same bit with the same material.

Step 4: Set the remaining parameters

As you work through the remaining setup options, there are a few things to keep in mind as you make your choices. Raster pocket clearing usually leaves a smoother surface in solid wood than Offset, **Image 3.21**. Offset works fine for other materials and is slightly faster, but may leave a spiral milling pattern at the bottom of the pocket. Run a few test cuts to determine your best option.

Climb cut is good in solid wood when chipping is a problem; otherwise Conventional usually leaves a smoother finish.

The Raster Angle allows you to set the raster direction, so it runs with or across the grain, or at an angle.

The Profile Pass provides a final cleanup cut around the perimeter of the rastered pocket—selecting Last works well in most situations. Pocket Allowance lets you machine the pocket oversize or undersize in the X and Y directions. Using a Ramp Plunge is recommended for most situations because it eases the bit into the material. Complete the toolpath setup by filling in the Name field and clicking on the Calculate button, which also closes the window.

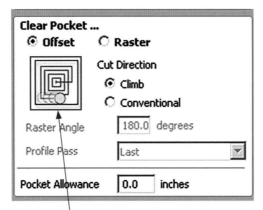

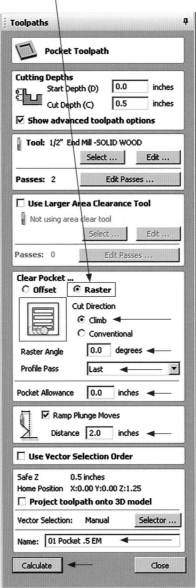

Image 3.21: The main *Toolpath* menu contains a variety of settings. It's good to run down the list to verify or change those that are important to your particuar setup.

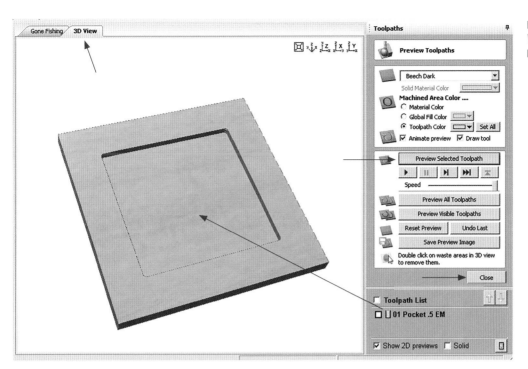

Image 3.22: The *3-D View* tab allows you to preview the toolpath.

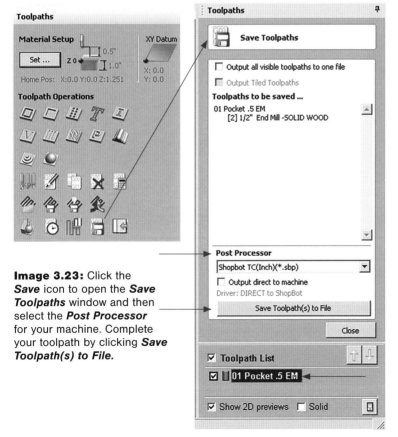

Image 3.23: Click the *Save* icon to open the *Save Toolpaths* window and then select the *Post Processor* for your machine. Complete your toolpath by clicking *Save Toolpath(s) to File.*

Step 5: Preview the toolpath

In the 3-D View tab, click the Selected Toolpath button to view a simulation of the tool cutting, the material, and the final results, **Image 3.22**. Then click Close to return to the main Toolpath menu.

Before moving on, save the cutting toolpath cutting file, **Image 3.23**. To do so, select the toolpaths that you want to save and choose the Post Processor that matches your tool setup. The Post Processor converts the toolpaths to machine code. Click on Save Toolpath(s) to File and save your cutting file to your computer or a flash drive so you can transfer it to your CNC machine.

CHAPTER

4

Machine Setup

We're nearly ready to start cutting on the CNC machine! But before that can happen, we need to first set up and check a few things on the machine, so let's take a look at:

- **Job setup**

- **Material hold-down methods**

- **Zeroing the X, Y, and Z axes**

- **Testing a cutting file**

- **Spoilboard maintenance**

Job Setup

Machine setup actually starts in the CAD/ CAM software with Job Setup, **Image 4.1**. This includes entering the width, height, and thickness of your material, and the zero locations for the X, Y, and Z axes. This information carries through to the toolpath, so it's important to understand how it relates to your material and machine, **Image 4.2**.

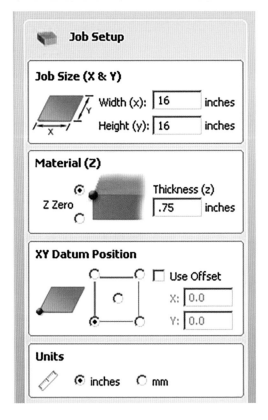

Image 4.1: The *Job Setup* in the CAD/ CAM software sets material parameters that carry through to the machine. Z-zeroing to the top of the material is common for V-carving and 3-D carving. Z-zeroing to the bottom of the material is useful when you're cutting all the way through the material, because it is not affected by variations in material thickness. Setting the *XY Datum Position* to the lower left or the center of the material are the two most frequently used locations.

Image 4.2: Your material can be attached any place on the table, as long as the datum position for zeroing the XY matches the setting you chose in in the *Job Setup.*

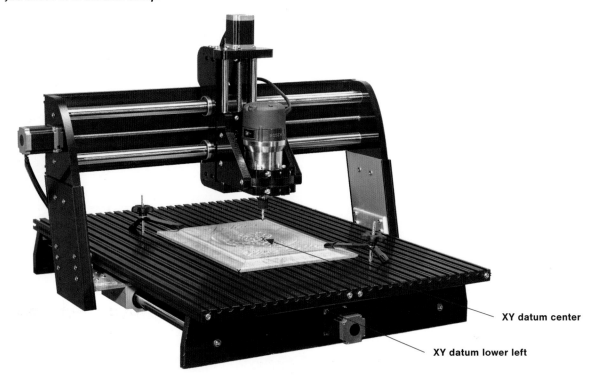

XY datum center

XY datum lower left

Material hold-down

There are many ways to secure your material to the machine. The method you choose depends on the machine you have, the material you're using, the kind of work you're doing, and what's fastest for you. The following methods are some of the most common and simplest to use.

If your CNC machine has T-track, you can use hold-down clamps to secure your work to the table, **Image 4.3**. This is a fast and easy way to get your stock on and off the machine. As long as you properly tightened them, they will solidly hold the work in place. Some CNC users use shop-made wooden hold-downs, instead of metal hold-downs. This minimizes the risk to your bit, although colliding with the wooden hold-down may still break the bit. If you use metal hold-downs be sure they're aluminum, not steel. Aluminum will do less damage to your cutter if they collide.

Hot glue has plenty of holding power for many types of CNC work, **Image 4.4**. Make sure your spoilboard is clean and relatively smooth. Dust on the spoilboard will prevent the hot glue from bonding. Choose an area on the spoilboard that doesn't have a lot of deep cuts from previous projects. These cuts minimize contact between your project and the spoilboard, weakening the glue bond.

Apply the hot melt glue as a fillet along the edge of the project. Hold your material firmly to the CNC table while applying the glue. Do not put hot melt glue between the

Image 4.3: T-track and hold-down clamps provide a very fast means of getting material on and off the CNC table.

Image 4.4: Hot glue is an effective way to secure work to the spoilboard. Apply it at the inside corner created by your work and the spoilboard.

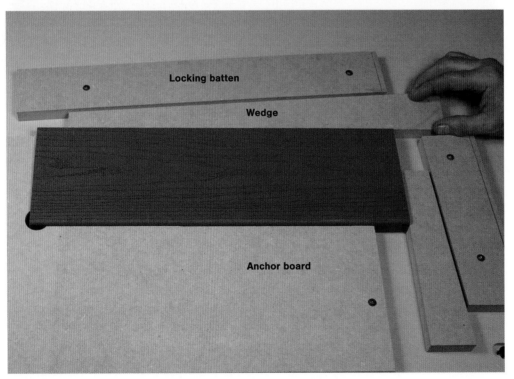

Locking batten

Wedge

Anchor board

Image 4.5: Wedges allow you to secure and remove your material quickly. They work great for runs of identically sized pieces that need to be precisely located. NOTE: *Do not* use this jig with upcut bits; this may pull the material up and out of the jig and cause injury to the operator or others nearby.

Image 4.6: Screws are a very secure hold-down technique, but there is a risk of hitting screws when machining. To avoid this risk, add the locations for the screws into your design file to make sure they are out of the cutting path.

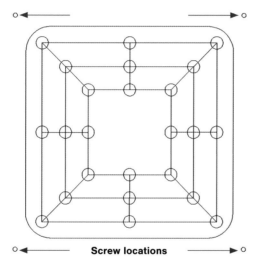

Screw locations

When you're cutting several pieces of the same size, you can take advantage of wedges to hold them in place, **Image 4.5**. Secure an anchor board to the table and then make a right angle cut in it with your CNC. This gives you a precise location to align your material. Place your project material into the anchor board. Position the wedges and locking battens. Screw the locking battens in place. Wedges with a 5° angle work well. The battens can be straight boards since they can be positioned on the table to match the angle on the wedges. MDF is great for the anchor board, locking battens, and wedges.

A medium rap with a mallet on the wide end of the wedge will hold the material in place. A rap on the other end of the wedge will free the wedge when you're finished cutting. Wedges provide excellent lateral pressure but provide no downward pressure, so don't use this hold-down method when using an upcut spiral router bit.

Screws provide a very secure way to attach your material to the CNC table. However, you must be certain that the screws are not in the cutting path. The easiest way to keep the screws out of the cutting path is to incorporate their locations into your project design, **Image 4.6**. Place ⅛"-diameter circles wherever you need screws. Set up a Pocket Toolpath and a V-bit set to a cutting depth of ⅛". The goal is to dimple the board lightly at each screw location.

back of your project and the spoilboard or table. Hot glue is very thick, and using it between the board and table will likely cause your material to be higher on one end than the other, resulting in an uneven cut.

Remove the board by slicing the bead of hot glue with a utility knife and lifting the board. Peel and shear any remaining glue from the table with a sharp chisel or putty knife.

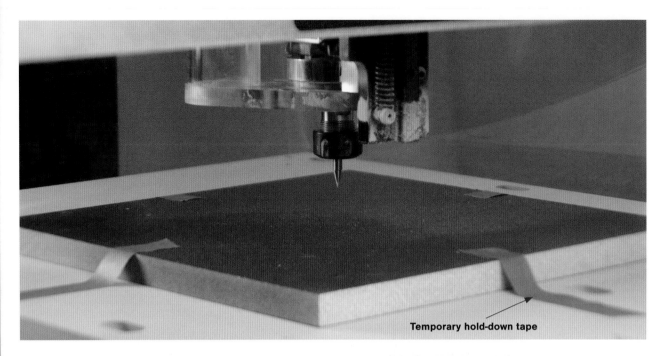

Temporary hold-down tape

At your machine, fasten your material to the CNC table with masking tape or spots of hot melt glue, **Image 4.7.** The masking tape is temporary but will hold the material well enough for the light cuts required to dimple the board. The tape is not needed when dimpling large sheets of material, since the weight of the material will be enough to hold it in place. After making the dimples, drill, countersink, and drive screws at each location. The screws may cause the spoilboard to pucker up, which can lift the material and affect cutting depths. If this becomes a problem for your project, countersink the back of the material to give the pucker a place to expand into.

Image 4.7:
Temporarily secure your material to the worktable, then use a V-bit or small straight bit to cut shallow dimples in the material to mark the locations for the screws. In some materials, it may then be necessary to predrill and countersink the screw holes.

Zeroing the axes

Before cutting you need to zero the X, Y, and Z axes. This process provides a consistent reference point between the machine, your material, and the router bit. Most CNC machines have built-in software routines for zeroing the axes. The XY-zeroing routine is usually automatic, while the Z routine often requires operator involvement.

Zero the Z axis

The Z axis can be zeroed using a touch plate or manually. We'll look at both methods. The first step is to check your design program and determine where you set the Z-zero. If Z-zero is at the top of the board, you'll zero the Z axis to the top surface of your material. If the Z-zero is set to the bottom of the board, zero the Z axis to the spoilboard of the CNC machine. You'll need to reset the Z-zero each time you change router bits or use a material of different thickness.

Z-zero touch plates consist of a metal plate and an electrical lead, **Image 4.8**. They take the guesswork out of the Z-zeroing process. The first step is to position the touch plate on your Z-zero surface and connect the electrical lead to the CNC machine. Be sure the router bit is directly over the touch plate, **Image 4.9**. Locate the Z-zero control on the control pendant or within the control software for your machine and start the zeroing process. The bit will automatically move

Image 4.8: Z-zeroing touch plates come in a variety of configurations, but have similar characteristics; a metal plate and an electrical lead.

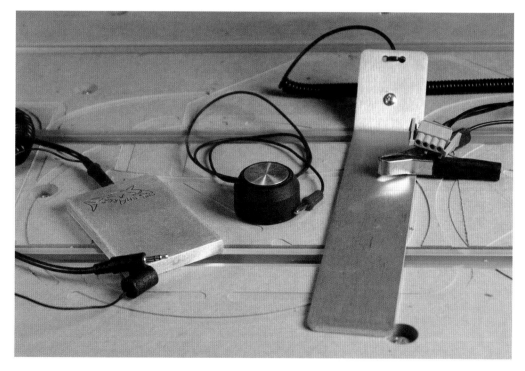

Image 4.9: To zero the Z axis, place the touch plate on top of the material for "top of material" zeroing, or on the spoilboard for "bottom of material" zeroing. The Z-zeroing routine in the control software or with the pendant will lower the non-spinning bit until it touches the plate. The control software is calibrated to know the thickness of the plate, so this is an accurate and quick way to set the Z-zero height for a cutting file.

down toward the touch plate until it makes contact, then stop and move back up. The control software has the thickness of the plate programmed into it, so your CNC machine is now accurately calibrated to the surface of your material or table.

When manually zeroing the Z axis, the first step is to turn on incremental or fixed stepping in the control software. Check your tool's manual on how to set up incremental/fixed stepping. The step setting controls how far the bit travels each time you ask it to move. By making the step a small number you have greater control over the bit movement, and will be able to fine-tune the Z-zero position. It also prevents you from driving the bit into your material. With a bit installed, move it toward the workpiece or table. Take your time as you near the zero surface. Place a piece of paper on the zero surface and

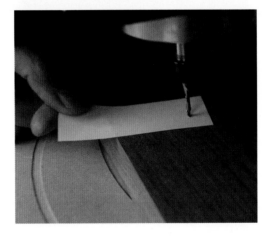

Image 4.10: The Z axis can also be manually zeroed by jogging the router bit down to the work until you've gently squeezed a piece of paper between the bit and the zero surface. Use the manual command in the control software to jog the Z down in small increments.

stop when there's slight pressure from the bit on the paper, **Image 4.10**. You should be able to slide the paper but feel a little resistance. Use your control pendant or software to set this location as Z-zero.

Zeroing X and Y

The XY-zero location can be set any place on your machine, but it must be the same as the XY Datum Position you selected in Job Setup of the CAD/CAM software. Once

Image 4.11: To set the XY-zero position to the center of your material, center the bit over a mark on your material and then press the **XY-Zero** button on the control pendant or zero the XY axis using the control software on the computer.

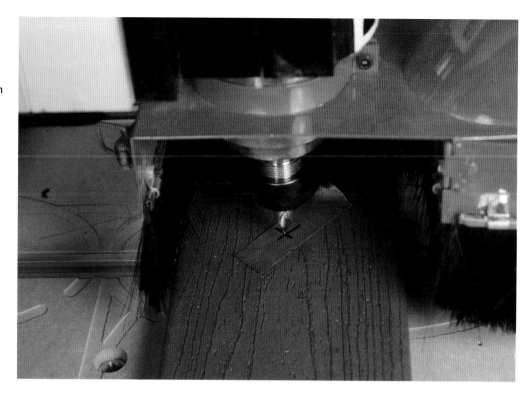

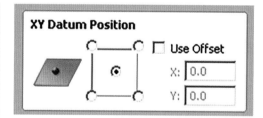

you've positioned the spindle over the center or lower left of your material, use the control pendant or control software to set this as the XY-zero location. The two most common are center XY-zeroing, **Image 4.11**, and lower left XY-zeroing, **Image 4.12**.

Test cutting your files

Before cutting your project on your CNC, it's a good idea to double-check it in the CAD/CAM program to make sure everything is correct. VCarve Pro software has a great Preview Toolpath function that lets you see a virtual cut of your CNC project on your computer. Other CNC control software packages have similar preview toolpath features. But these are virtual views only, and sometimes it's helpful to run the cutting file on your machine and watch it move—but without cutting the material. This is called "air cutting." Some CNC control software packages include this function, but it's easy to set up any machine for an air cut. The most important step in setting up an air cut is to set the Z-zero at a distance above your material and clamps, so when you run the file, the bit won't touch anything. Your CNC will go through all the movements in the cutting file, allowing you to watch for any unexpected movements. One more physical test that you can run is to cut your

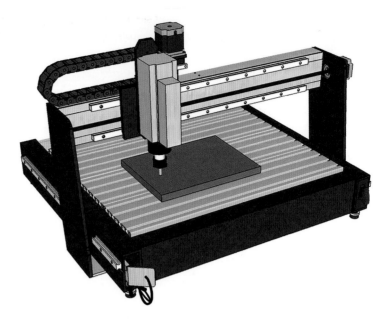

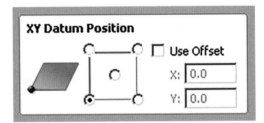

Image 4.12:
XY-zeroing to the lower left of your material uses the same steps as XY-zeroing to the center, except you position the spindle over the lower left corner of your material.

parts in an inexpensive material such as foam. All this testing may seem excessive, and for some files it may be, but testing is a great way to avoid making the common design, toolpath, and setup mistakes that every CNC user makes at some point along the way.

Spoilboard maintenance

Over time, the spoilboard on your machine will become grooved and rough, **Image 4.13**. Resurfacing the spoilboard is a regular part of CNC maintenance and should be done before the roughness interferes with cutting accuracy. You only need to remove enough material to restore its usefulness. You can skip over a few of the deeper cuts if they're not causing a problem, or you can rout them out and glue in a patch. But eventually, your spoilboard will become too thin to be useful. At that point, you need to replace it, or simply glue a new spoilboard on top of the old one. That works fine on most machines and creates a little extra thickness, which can be useful if you regularly use screws to hold down your material. Surfacing the spoilboard is done using a large Pocket Toolpath that you can generate from your CAD/CAM program, or from the control software of some machines, **Image 4.14**.

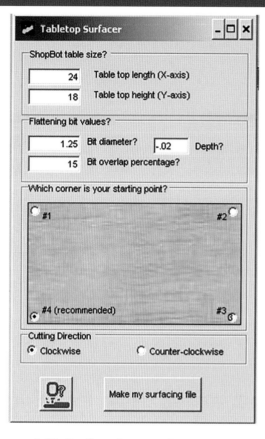

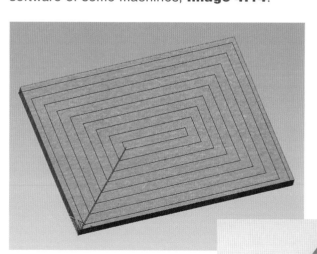

Image 4.13: Spoilboards eventually become grooved and need to be renewed using a large surfacing bit.

Image 4.14: Table surfacing functions are included with some control software, or you can create your own spoilboard surfacing file by drawing and toolpathing a rectangle the size of your spoilboard in your CAD/CAM program.

CHAPTER

5

Project Materials

CNC routers can be used to cut nearly any material, including wood, plastics, aluminum, foam, brass, and more. If equipped with special cutting tools, you can also use it to engrave glass and granite, or to cut cardboard or vinyl. The possibilities are nearly endless. Whatever material you choose, it's important to know its working characteristics. Some woods chip more than others and some plastics melt easier than others; knowing the difference has a big effect on the success of your CNC cutting. Let's look at some of the mainstream materials you can use.

- **Lumber and wood products**
- **Composite building materials**
- **Plastics and foams**

Image 5.1: Hardwoods such as cherry, walnut, and maple are good for 3-D carvings because they hold detail well.

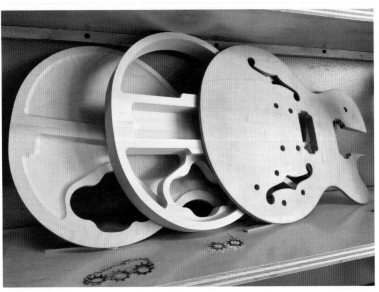

Image 5.2: Solid wood is hard to beat for its beauty, strength, and working characteristics when you have special projects to build like this guitar.

Solid wood

CNCs can cut both hardwoods and softwoods. If you can rout it with your handheld router or router table, you can rout it on a CNC. Woods such as walnut, maple, cherry, and poplar work well for CNC carving projects, **Images 5.1 and 5.2**. Pine and oak, because of their coarse grain texture, don't work as well for detailed carving. Cedar is a good choice for outdoor signs, **Image 5.3**. It's naturally weather resistant and cuts fairly well. Cedar is a softwood, so not a good choice for projects that are highly detailed, as it doesn't hold the detail well. The working characteristics of wood that affect the cut quality with a handheld router also apply to the CNC. So, if a wood chips, splinters, tears out, or gets fuzzy on your router table, it will likely do the same on a CNC. But the bit you choose

Image 5.3: Cedar is a good choice for outdoor signs. It's naturally rot and weather resistant and holds paint well. Or, if left unfinished, it takes on a nice gray weathered look.

along with the feed and speed rates will also have an effect. So, run some tests to find out what combinations work best for your application.

Image 5.4: MDF is a good choice for painted projects. It carves easily and can be finished to look like almost any material. This CNC-carved MDF plaque was sealed with a couple coats of shellac, lightly sanded, then coated with copper-colored spray paint. A top coat of green latex paint was then dabbed on with a rag to create an aged copper look.

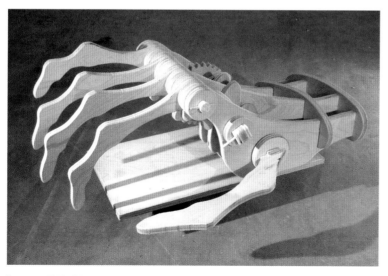

Image 5.5: Plywood is an extremely versatile material and widely available in a variety of grades and thicknesses.

Plywood and MDF

Woodworkers have a love/hate relationship with MDF. It's inexpensive, readily available, very flat, and paints great, **Image 5.4**. It's also heavy and creates a lot of dust, even with good dust collection. But, unlike solid wood, there is no grain direction and it machines easily on a CNC. This results in cuts that are crisp and clean. Unfortunately, raw MDF is ugly. Thankfully it takes paint well, and with a little work, it can be made to look great. Since MDF is available in 4' x 8' sheets, you won't need to glue pieces together to get large panels.

Plywood, like MDF, is available in large sheets, but has more structural strength and weighs less than MDF. The cross-grain layers in plywood give it a tremendous amount of rigidity that allows you to cut complex shapes without compromising the integrity of the material, **Image 5.5**.

The edges of most types of plywood look raw, but this doesn't matter for many types of projects, and some designers have found ways to highlight the edge as a design element in their projects.

Image 5.6: Composite decking is easy to machine. It's weather proof and has a wood grain texture that makes it a good choice for simple exterior signs.

Composite decking

Composite decking, like MDF, has no grain direction and cuts well. It's widely available at home centers under a variety of brand names. Since it's designed to be outside, no finish is required. The embossed grain pattern gives it the look of real wood, **Image 5.6**.

Plastics

Acrylic plastic cuts well on the CNC, but make sure to use a bit made for acrylics. Acrylic is relatively inexpensive and comes in a variety of colors and thickness, **Image 5.7**. It's highly chemical and weather resistant, making it a good choice for signs and parts exposed to harsh environments. The clear variety is very transparent and an excellent choice when visibility though the material is important. Acrylic is several times tougher than glass, yet not as tough as other plastics such as polycarbonate.

Polycarbonate is a strong durable plastic that is highly resistant to cracking and shattering. That's why it's used for motorcycle windshields, eyeglass lenses, and bullet-proof glass. It's several times stronger than acrylic, which means that you can cut shapes and parts that are tough

Image 5.7: When working with acrylics and other clear plastics, it's common to carve a reverse image into the back of the piece. This leaves the front smooth for a clean look.

Image 5.8: White PVC plastic trim board material is readily available at home centers. Applying a coat of paint before machining is a quick, inexpensive way to create a high contrast sign that can be used outside with no further finishing.

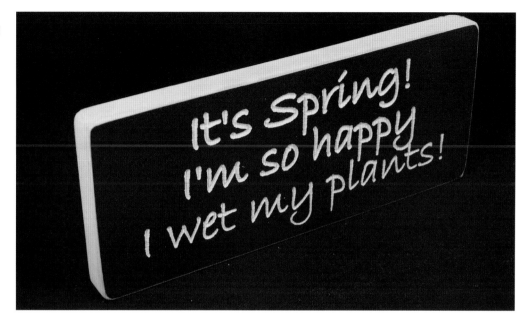

to damage. However, polycarbonate is several times more expensive than acrylic. Clear acrylic and polycarbonate sheets are both available at most home centers and hardware stores. Colored and thick varieties are available online and through plastic distributors.

PVC is used by home builders as house trim and available at most home centers. It's the same plastic used in PVC plumbing. PVC trim boards are usually only available in white, and in thickness and widths similar to building lumber, **Images 5.8 and** 5.9, but there are online sources for colored PVC board.

Image 5.9: You can also use your CNC to customize stock millwork. The parts of this PVC railing were machined to match those on an existing porch.

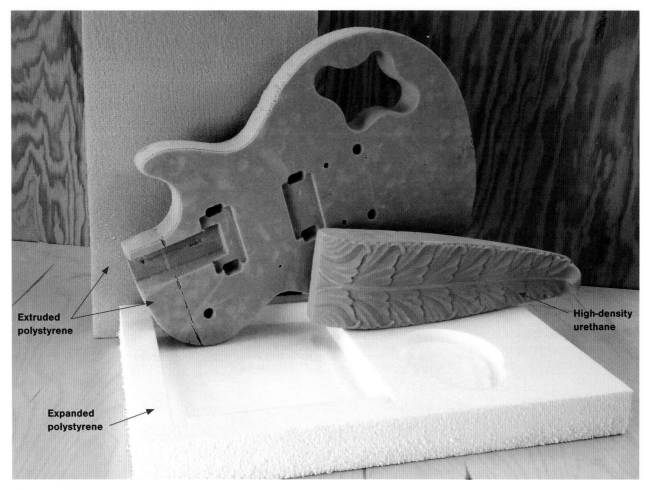

Extruded
polystyrene

High-density
urethane

Expanded
polystyrene

Image 5.10: Foam is easy to cut and is a good material for cutting tests and prop building. High-density urethane (HDU), extruded polystyrene (XPS), and expanded polystyrene (EPS) are a few of the many available. Each has its pros and cons, depending on your application.

Foams

Foam comes in a variety of types and grades, **Image 5.10**. There are inexpensive varieties that are useful for test cutting and lightweight temporary parts, and more expensive types used for sign making and industrial prototyping. When cutting any of these foams, a good dust collection system is essential because machining foam creates a lot of static-laden dust. Home centers generally carry two types— expanded polystyrene (EPS) and extruded polystyrene (XPS). EPS is typically white and has a beaded texture, like a coffee cup or foam cooler. It's the least expensive, but its beaded texture tends to leave a rough surface, though there are finer grades available from foam distributors. It's also available in blocks or thick sheets. The low-density, low-cost variety available at home centers has a coarsely beaded texture, but is still useful for test cutting and custom packaging.

The XPS that's available at home centers is typically colored (pink, blue, or yellow). It's more expensive than white EPS, but has a fine closed-cell texture that machines nicely.

Another type of foam, high-density urethane (HDU), comes in a variety of densities (pounds per cubic foot) from light to heavy. HDU is more expensive than polystyrene foams, but it has a very smooth texture with excellent machining characteristics. It's widely used for large exterior signs because it's weatherproof, lightweight (compared to wood), and easily finished with paint or other coatings. The heavier grades are used for prototyping parts. HDU foam is available from a variety of online vendors.

Aluminum and other non-ferrous metal can also be cut on most CNC routers. They require the right router bit, fine-tuned feeds and speeds, and a very solid hold-down method, but these materials will expand your CNC project options.

CHAPTER

6

Practice Project 1:

Basic Drawing & Toolpath Techniques

The instructions in this chapter will guide you through the steps of designing a V-carved plaque. The beauty of designing on a computer is that you can easily make changes , so don't be afraid to experiment with the design. In this project, you'll learn how to:

- **Set up a new project file**

- **Draw rectangles and create offsets**

- **Add text**

- **Create toolpaths for pocketing, profiling, and V-carving**

- **Add tabs**

Getting started

You'll learn a great deal about VCarve Pro and your CNC machine by creating and cutting the project in this chapter. If you're new to CNC, spend some time getting familiar with your CAD/CAM software before you start cutting. Understanding how to use the various CAD tools is an important part of learning how to design for CNC.

These are the tools that you will use to complete the CAD portion of this project.

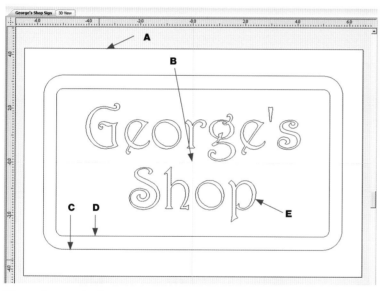

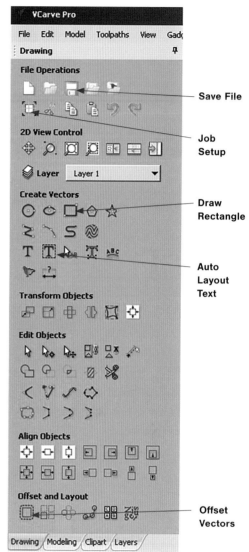

The primary design elements for this project include: (A) Material size, (B) *XY Datum Position,* also called the XY-zero location, (C) an outer rectangle with round corners, (D) an inner rectangle made using the *Offset Vector* tool, (E) and the *Auto Layout Text* feature.

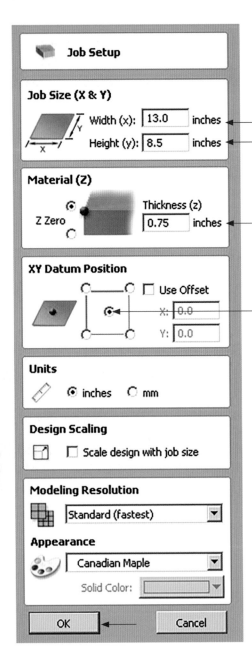

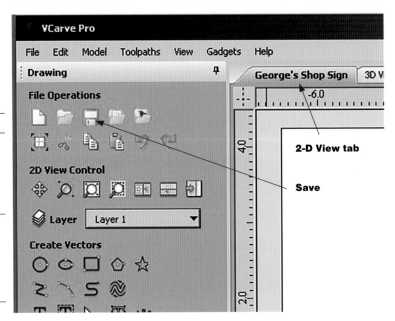

Step 2: Click the **Save** icon. Select a folder on your computer and give the file a name. The file name will then appear in 2-D view tab. The file you just saved is the design file, not to be confused with the toolpath/cutting file that you will later create and take to your tool.

Job Setup

Create a new file and use the Job Setup menu to set the workpiece dimensions, **Step 1**. We recommend that you stick with the dimensions provided because we know this recipe works for this project. Note that the Z-Zero is set to the top of the material, and the XY-zero (XY Datum Position) is set to the center of the workpiece. Choice of material or modeling resolution isn't critical. Now is a good time to save your design file to a folder on your computer, **Step 2**. It's also a good idea to save your file periodically while working with it, just in case your computer crashes. This file is your design file, not to be confused with the toolpath/cutting files that you will later create and take to your CNC tool.

Step 1: The **Job Setup** window is the starting point for any project. Start by setting the **Width (X), Height (Y),** and **Thickness (Z)** for your material. For this project, set the **XY Datum Position** to the center of the material. Click **OK** to save the settings.

Creating rectangles and offsets

Create a rectangle using the Draw Rectangle tool, **Step 3**. Use the center as the Anchor Point and set the X and Y positions to 0. Give the corners an external radius of .75". Set the width (X) to 11.5" and the height (Y) to 6.5". To save the settings, click Create.

Next, we want to create a "frame" by adding a slightly smaller rectangle. The easiest way to accomplish this is with the Offset Vectors tool, **Step 4**. Click on the existing rectangle to select it (it turns pink) and then choose the Offset Vectors tool. Select the Inwards/Left option, set the distance to .5" and click Offset. A new rectangle will appear, perfectly centered, within the existing rectangle.

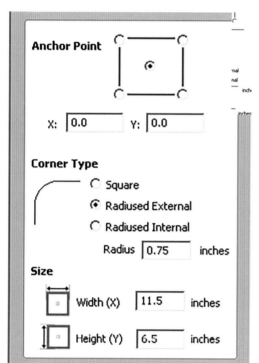

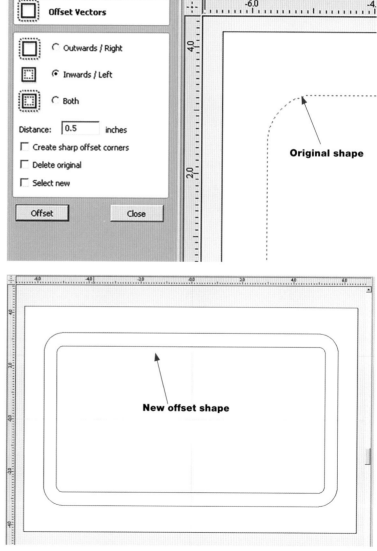

Step 3: Open the *Draw Rectangle* tool to create a rectangle with rounded corners. Match all these settings. Then click *Create* and *Close* to create the outer rectangle.

Step 4: The *Offset Vectors* tool is an easy way to create a duplicate shape that is larger or smaller than the original. Select the existing rectangle, then click *Offset* and *Close* to complete.

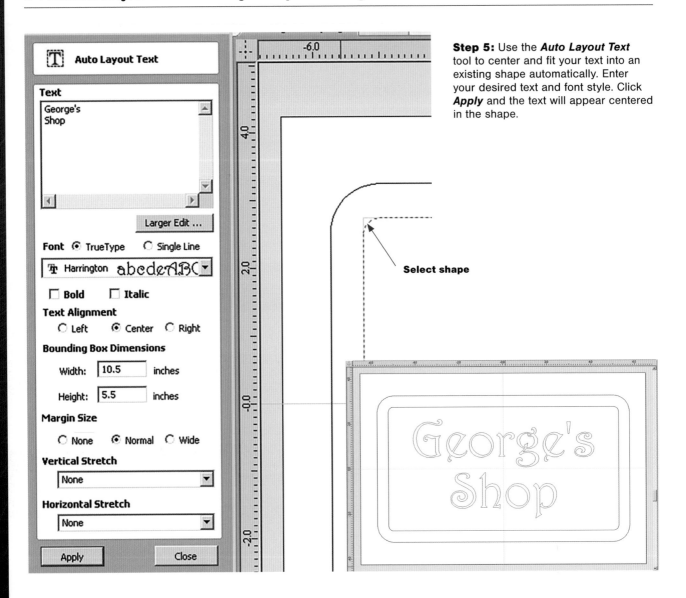

Step 5: Use the *Auto Layout Text* tool to center and fit your text into an existing shape automatically. Enter your desired text and font style. Click *Apply* and the text will appear centered in the shape.

Adding text

We'll turn this project into a sign by adding text, **Step 5**. Click on the inner rectangle to select it, and then click open the Auto Layout Text tool. Choose the font you'd like to use, and type the text you want into the Text box. The font used here, Harrington, may not be available on your computer, but you'll find a number of other fonts to choose from. Match the remaining settings, select the inner rectangle, then click Apply; the text will appear centered and scaled to fit your workspace. To make changes to the text, select the text and reopen the Auto Layout Text tool. You can adjust the text, font, style, and size until you like the look of what you have.

The design part of this project is now complete.

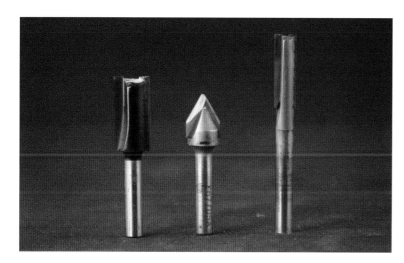

This project calls for three bits (from left to right): ½"-diameter straight bit, 60° V-bit, and a ¼"-diameter straight bit.

The three toolpaths needed for this project are also three of the most commonly used CNC toolpaths. Each is set up slightly differently and we'll take a look at those settings in the following steps.

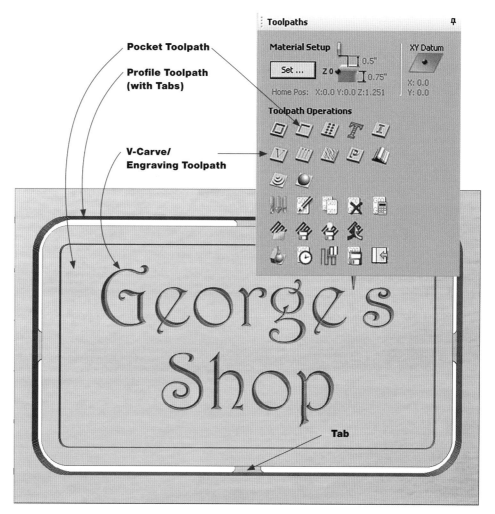

Pocket Toolpath

Profile Toolpath (with Tabs)

V-Carve/ Engraving Toolpath

Tab

Create toolpaths

The next step is to create the toolpaths that will turn your design into a reality. We'll first create the pocket or recess in the center of the sign, **Step 6**. Click on the Toolpath tab and open the Pocket Toolpath function. Select the inner rectangle then set the Cut Depth to .15". Next, go to Tool and Select and choose a ½" End Mill from the Tool Database (library). Setting the Stepover to 40 percent is common for

Step 6: Open the **Pocket Toolpath** window and select the inner rectangle. Set the **Cutting Depths** then click **Select** to open the **Tool Database.** Select **½" End Mill** and match the rest of settings in the **Tool Database** window. Click **OK** to save the tool settings. Match the remaining settings in the main window, then click **Calculate** and **Close** to complete setup.

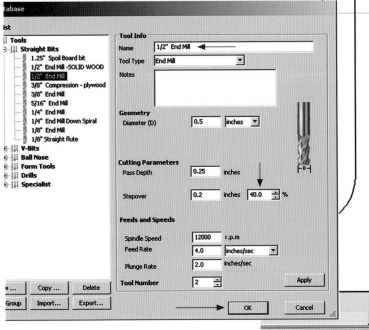

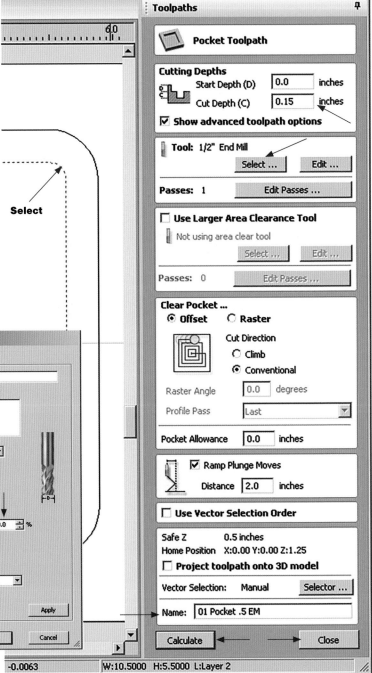

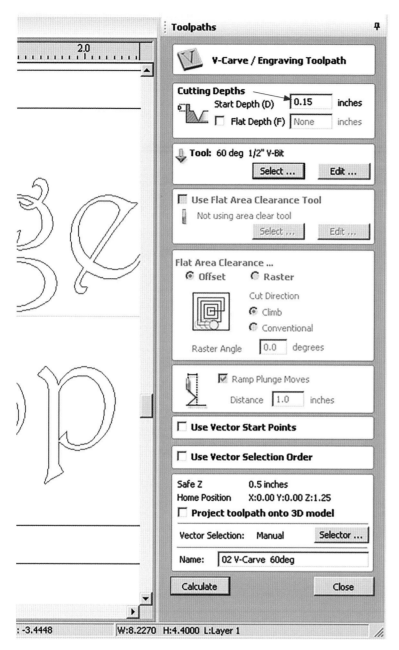

pocket cutting. Stepover is the amount the bit moves over for each new pass—just like when mowing a lawn. Match the rest of the settings in the Tool Database window, click OK to save the settings, then match the rest of the settings in the Pocket Toolpath window. Complete the setup by giving the toolpath a name. You'll find it easier to keep track of the toolpaths and your bit choices if you incorporate cut type and bit into the name. Numbering the toolpaths also helps keep them organized. For example, a good name for this toolpath would be 01 Pocket .5 EM. Then, click Calculate.

The letters are next. Click on the text to select it, then choose the V-Carve/Engraving Toolpath, **Step 7.** Under Cutting Depths set the Start Depth to .15", the depth we used to cut the pocket in the previous step. This tells the CNC machine to start the cut at a level lower than the top surface of the board, which is considered zero. Under Tools choose 60° V-Bit from the bit library. Name the toolpath, then click Calculate.

Step 7: Use the *V-Carve/Engraving Toolpath* to cut the letters. Make sure to set the *Start Depth* to the depth of the recessed pocket we created in the previous step. Match the remaining settings and click *Calculate* to save.

Cutting the outer rectangle is the final toolpath for this project. Select the outer rectangle and open the Profile Toolpath tool, **Step 8**. Under Cutting Depths set the Cut Depth to .77". We want the router bit to go completely through the material, but only by the small amount of .02" (¹⁄₃₂" or so). Under Tool, choose the ¼" End Mill router bit. Make sure the bit you're using has a long enough cutting length to go completely through the workpiece. Under Passes click on Edit Passes and set the number to 5. Under Machine Vectors select Outside/Right. This option tells the CNC where to cut relative to the line; outside, inside, or centered on the line.

Since we've set the 2-D Profile Toolpath to cut all the way through, we need to do something to prevent the workpiece from breaking completely free while cutting. This is accomplished by using tabs. Scroll

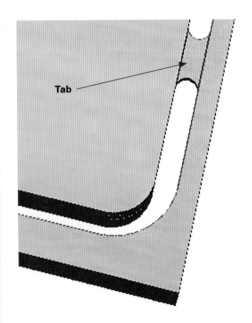

Tab

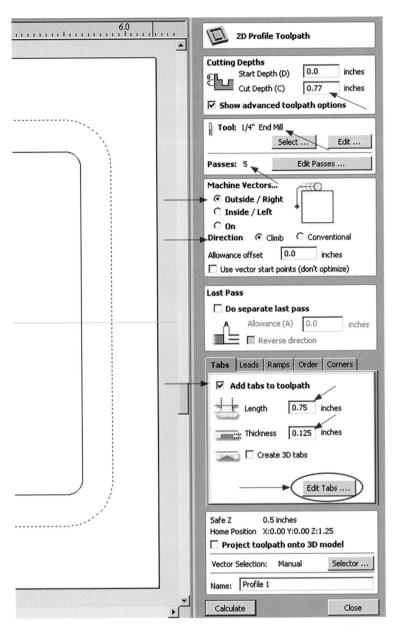

Step 8: Use the *2-D Profile Toolpath* to cut the exterior shape of the project. This step involves setting several parameters. Start by matching all the settings above. Then click on the *Edit Tabs* button to open the *Toolpath Tabs* window.

Adding *Tabs* to the *Profile Toolpath* prevents the project from breaking free during the machining process.

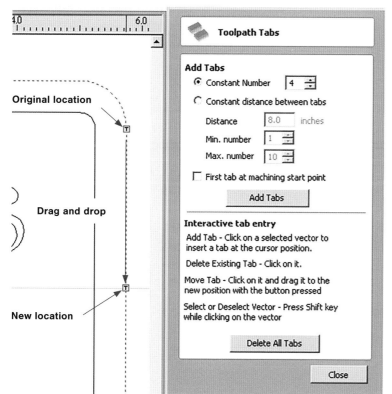

Step 9: Set *Constant Number* to 4 for this project and click *Add Tabs*; you'll then see the tabs appear on your design. To move a tab, click on it and drag it to a new location. It's best for tabs to be on straight edges, not on curves. Click *Close* to save your settings and exit the window.

Step 10: To complete the *Profile Toolpath* setup, name it and click *Calculate.*

A warning will pop up because the cutting depth for this project was set deeper than the thickness of the material. Click *OK* for this project.

down to the Tabs box. Check the box next to Add Tabs to Toolpath, and click Edit Tabs. A Toolpath Tabs box will appear, **Step 9**. This is where you adjust the location of the tabs. Match the settings shown and click Add Tabs. The tabs appear on the outside rectangle as small yellow boxes.

Cleaning up a tab on a straight edge of a project is usually easier than on a curve. So if tabs in your design appear in an inconvenient spot, they can easily be moved by clicking and dragging them to a new location. Deleting or adding tabs can also be easily accomplished with a few

mouse clicks. Four tabs for this project are sufficient. Click Close when you're done editing the tabs. Complete the toolpath by filling in the Name field and clicking on Calculate, **Step 10**. A warning will pop up because the cutting depth for this project was set deeper than the thickness of the material. Setting the cutting depth slightly deeper than the thickness of the material is a common practice and is done to make sure the router bit cuts all the way through the material. But if you are working directly on a metal or non-sacrificial machine bed, you should add a board, such as ¼" MDF

Step 11: Click *Preview All Toolpaths* to preview the toolpaths. You can view the preview from different angles by clicking on the view icons at the top of the window. Click Close to return to the main Toolpath window.

under your project to avoid damaging the bed of your machine.

Now it's time for one of the most exciting, and coolest, parts of designing on VCarve Pro; making a virtual cut. Open the Preview Toolpaths window and then click on Preview All Toolpaths, **Step 11.** Previewing the toolpaths gives you a virtual look at what your project will look like after it's cut. Use this opportunity to make certain everything is coming out the way you want. If you click on the rendering, hold down the left mouse button, and move the

mouse, you can turn the project in different directions. Clicking on Reset Preview will remove the previous preview cuts from the material so you can preview it again. This is useful if you want to make changes to your design or toolpaths and want to preview it again. You can also increase or decrease the speed of the virtual cutting action by moving the Speed slider. Running the preview at a slower speed may allow you to more readily see errors in the toolpaths.

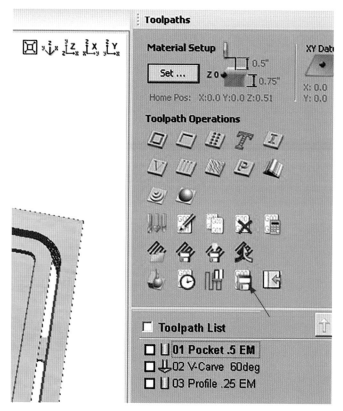

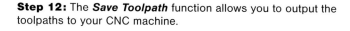

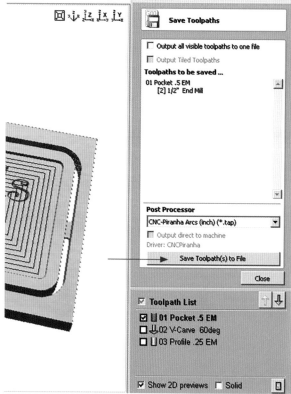

Step 12: The *Save Toolpath* function allows you to output the toolpaths to your CNC machine.

Step 13: Several post processors are available within the VCarve software. Choose the correct one for your machine. Toolpaths are commonly saved on a flash drive that is then taken to the CNC machine.

Saving toolpaths

When the design and toolpaths are correct, save the toolpaths so you can output them to your CNC machine. Select the toolpath you want to save, and then click on the Save Toolpath icon, **Step 12**. The VCarve Pro software contains post processors for many different CNC machines. Choose the post processor for your machine, and then click Save Toolpath(s) to File, **Step 13**. This will open a window that allows you to navigate to the folder or device where you want to save the toolpath.

Machining your project

Secure your board to the CNC bed and zero the X, Y, and Z axes, **Step 14**. Since the profile cut goes all the way through, be sure you have a spoilboard in place. Make certain you have the correct bit installed and make the pocket cut, **Step 15**. Install the V-bit, zero the Z axis to the original surface of the board, and machine the letters, **Step 16**. Since we set the start depth at .15", the V-Carve/Engraving Toolpath will automatically drop down and cut on the surface of the pocketed area.

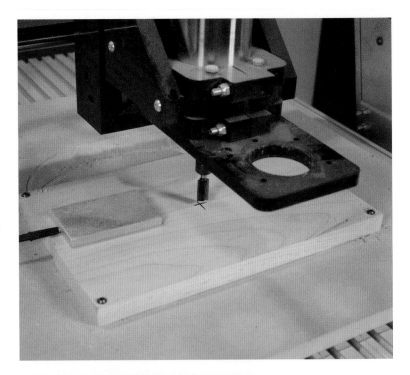

Step 14: To prepare for cutting this project, secure your work to the spoilboard and install the router bit for the **Pocket Toolpath.**

Step 15: The pocket cut will create a recessed area in the center of your board.

Step 16: Install the V-bit. Zero the Z to the top of the board, not in the recess. V-bits come in different angles (30, 60, 90, 120) and it's worth experimenting with the various bits to see the effects.

Install the straight bit for the profile cut. Zero the Z axis, and run the cutting file for the Profile Toolpath, **Step 17**. Remove your project from the CNC machine and use a bandsaw or handsaw to cut through the tabs. Sand the tabs flush and finish sand the entire sign. Your first CNC project is complete!

Step 17: The project is cut and ready to be removed from the CNC machine, sanded, and finished.

CHAPTER

7

Practice Project 2:

3-D Carving & Raised Lettering

This project reinforces what you learned in the previous project and adds some new techniques. In this project, you'll learn how to:

- **Create V-carved raised letters**
- **Insert 3-D clipart**
- **Move and resize objects (parts of your design)**
- **Create 3-D roughing and finishing toolpaths**

Getting started

This project adds to the design techniques of the previous project with several new CAD tools plus raised V-carved lettering and a carved 3-D model.

These are the tools that you will use to complete the CAD portion of this project.

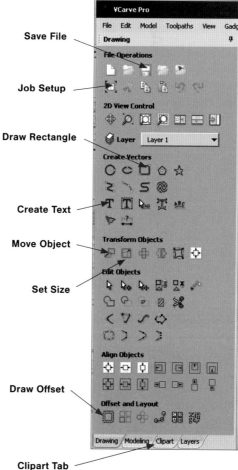

- Save File
- Job Setup
- Draw Rectangle
- Create Text
- Move Object
- Set Size
- Draw Offset
- Clipart Tab

3-D Clipart

The design elements for this project are the same as Project 1, with the addition of a piece 3-D clipart.

Job Setup

Start this project by creating a new file and entering the material dimensions, **Step 1**. The blank for this project is ¾" x 8½" x 13", so set the Width to 13", the Height to 8.5", and the Thickness to .75". Z-Zero from the top of the material. Place the XY Datum Position in the center.

Use the Draw Rectangle tool to create a rectangle that's 6.5" x 11.5" with Radiused external corners, **Step 2**. The corner radius is .75". Center the rectangle on the workpiece. Use the Offset Selected Vectors tool to create a second rectangle .5" inside the first rectangle.

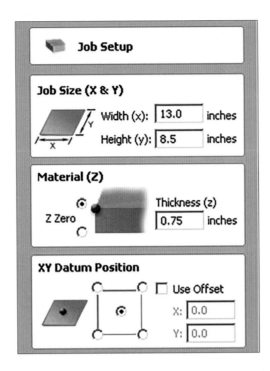

Step 1: The *Job Setup* window is the starting point for any project. Carefully measure the thickness of your piece and enter it. Match the remaining settings and save the design file to your computer. The details for saving a design file are covered in Project 1.

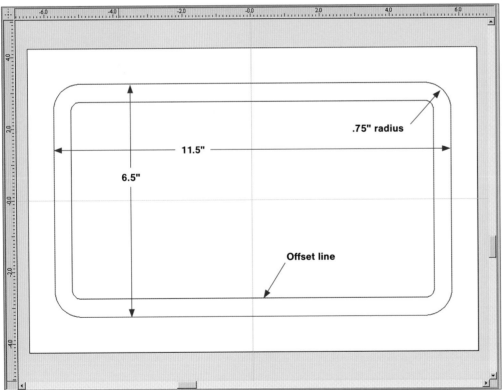

Step 2: Use the *Draw Rectangle* tool to create the outer rectangle and the *Offset* tool for the inner rectangle.

Add text

Use the Create Text tool to add text to the drawing, **Step 3**. Pick a font that you like. Set the text height to 1". Click on the Center placement option and click Apply. Use the Move Selection tool, **Step 4**, to place the text in the left half of the plaque. Any object in your design can be precisely positioned using this Move Selection tool. Converting this text to raised text will be done with the toolpath setup.

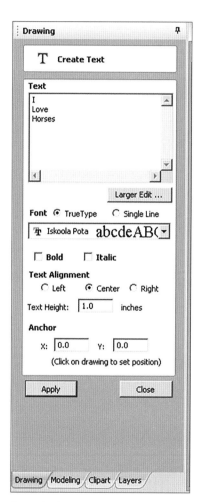

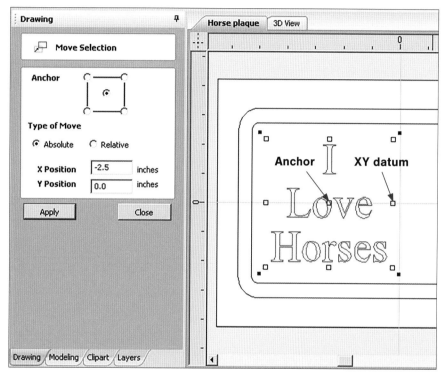

Step 4: Open the *Move Selection* window. Select the text and match the settings above. The *Anchor* point and *X* and *Y Position* settings are relative to the XY datum (zero) location. Complete the move by clicking *Apply* and *Close.* The text will then shift to the location shown above.

Step 3: Open the *Create Text* window. Enter desired words in the *Text* box, pick a *True Type Font,* select *Text Alignment Center*, set the *Text Height* to 1", then click *Apply* and *Close. Single Line* fonts are used for engraving and do not work with the *V-Carve/ Engraving Toolpath.*

Add 3-D clipart

There is a large library of 3-D clipart included with VCarve Pro. It provides an easy way to add a lot of visual interest to your project. Click on the Clipart tab on the lower left side of the screen, **Step 5**. When the new window opens click on Clipart at the top of the screen. Spend some time browsing through the available clipart. For this project click on Animals and you'll see the Cantering Arabian. Double-click on the horse in the center column (Cantering Arabian 50099 B.v3m) and it will appear in your drawing.

Centering and resizing objects

Open the Move Selection tool to precisely center the clipart in the right half of the plaque, **Step 6**. You can also hover the cursor over the center portion of the object until it turns into a four-way arrow and then drag and drop the object to a new location. This is not as precise, but it's quicker and particularly handy when you just want to move an object out of the way while doing other work.

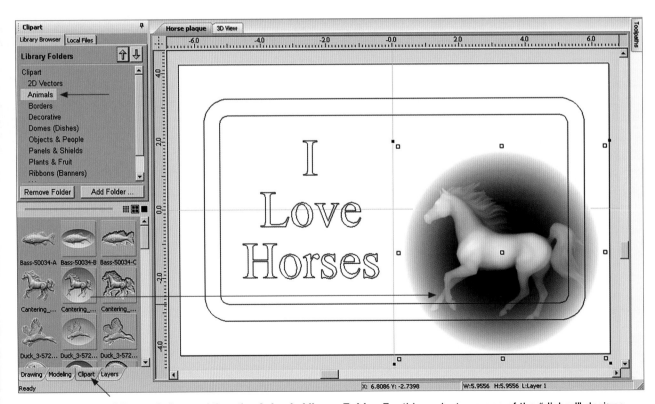

Step 5: Open the ***Clipart*** window and then the ***Animals Library Folder.*** For this project use one of the "dished" designs from the center column. Click/hold, drag, and drop the clipart to a location on the right side of the project. You can also just double-click the clipart to place it in the center of your drawing.

Step 6: Open the *Move Selection* window again and match the settings shown above. Click *Apply* and *Close* to complete the move. The object must be "selected" for the *Move* settings to have an effect. You can tell when an object is selected because it usually changes color (darker gray for clipart) and edit handles appear around its perimeter and center.

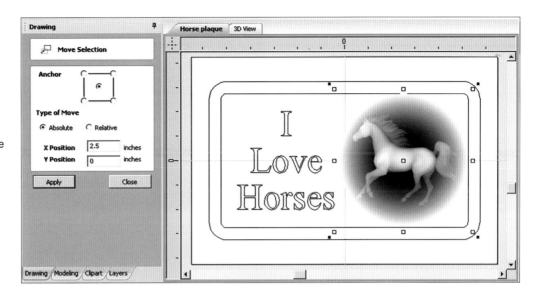

Step 7: Open the *Set Size* window. Set the *Anchor* point to center. This keeps the center of the object at the same location we set in Step 6. Next check the *Link XY* and *Auto Scale Z* boxes. Checking these boxes maintains the object's X, Y, and Z proportions. Enter the dimensions above, and click *Apply* and *Close* to complete this step.

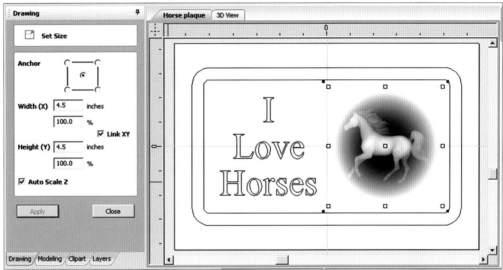

Resizing the clipart can be done by placing your cursor over one of the corner handles. The cursor will turn into a diagonal arrow. Click and hold the left mouse button and drag the square to change the clipart size. To precisely resize an object, use the Set Size tool, **Step 7**. This allows you to enter the exact dimensions for an object. If you want the item to stay proportional in both directions, check the Link XY checkbox and enter either the X or Y dimension. The other dimension will automatically fill in. This would also be a good time to save your file again by clicking the Save icon in the main menu.

Toolpaths

We'll use four router bits on this project. You can substitute straight bits for the spiral cutters, but if you use a different diameter bit, be sure to select the correct cutter when you're creating the toolpath. Create the Profile Toolpath for the exterior of the project using the same techniques we used in the previous chapter. Use a ⅜" bit and set the toolpath to cut slightly through the work; also, use tabs.

To carve the letters, select the text and the inner rectangle. Select the V-Carve/Engraving Toolpath, **Step 8**. Check Flat Depth, and set the depth to .18". Select the 60° ½" V-Bit from the Tool Database. Check Use Flat Area Clearance Tool and select the ⅜" End Mill bit. This arrangement tells the software to remove most of the waste with the ⅜" bit, and then detail the cut with the 60° bit. Complete the V-Carve/Engraving

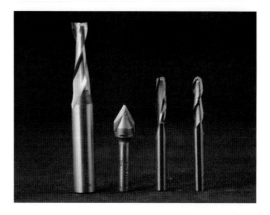

The four router bits for this project are a ⅜" diameter upcut straight bit, 60° V-bit, ¼" diameter upcut straight bit, and ¼" ballnose.

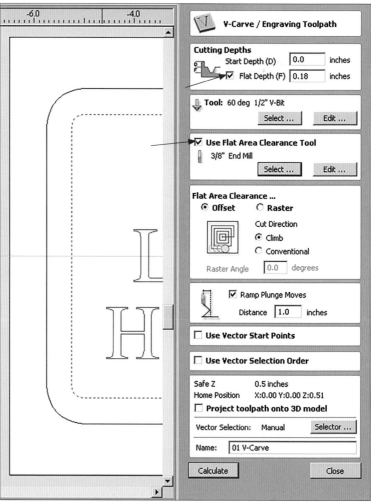

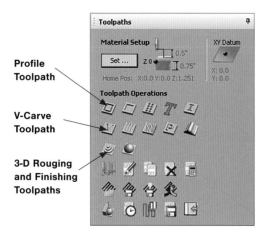

Here are toolpaths needed for this project. Notice that we're not using the *2-D Pocket Toolpath* this time. Instead, we'll use a special option inside the *V-Carve/Engraving Toolpath* to create the pocket.

Step 8: Open the *V-Carve/Engraving Toolpath* window. Select the text and the inner rectangle by holding down the *Shift* key on your keyboard and clicking on each part. Match the remaining settings, add text to the *Name* field, and then click *Calculate*.

Toolpath by checking Ramp Plunge Moves. Ramp distance should be 1". Name the file and click Calculate. Notice that two toolpaths were created. Preview these two toolpaths, **Steps 9 and 10**, to see how they work together to create the raised lettering. This raised V-carving technique works for shapes other than letters too.

Step 9: The *01 V-Carve [Pocket] Toolpat* was created with the *Use Flat Area Clearance* tool in Step 8. When you get to your machine, run the *Pocket Toolpath* before the *V-Carve/ Engraving Toolpath.*

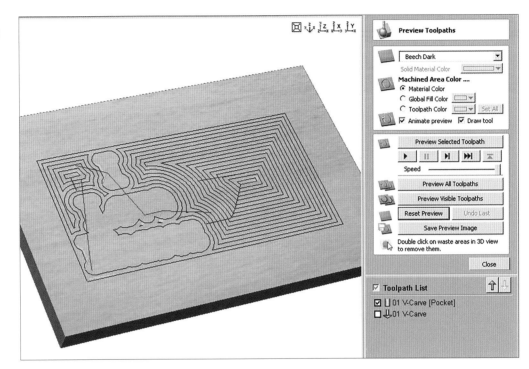

Step 10: Click *Preview Toolpaths* to see how this setup creates raised V-carved letters. The raised letters are a result of selecting both the rectangle and the text together when creating the *V-Carve/ Engraving Toolpath.* This change moves the cutting area from inside the letters to outside the letters.

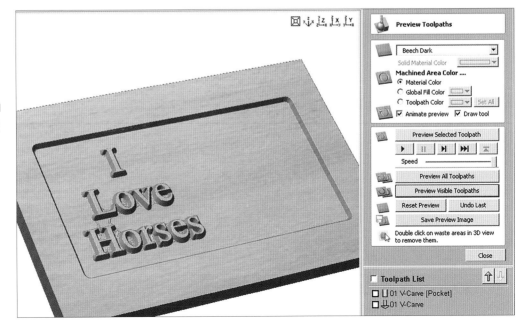

Next, we'll work on the toolpaths for the 3-D clipart. Since we're creating a pocket within the small rectangle, we need to position the clipart at the correct depth. Select the clipart and then open the Material Setup window by clicking on the Set button at the top of the main Toolpath menu, **Step 11**. In the Material Setup window, check the button for Gap Above Model, and enter .18". This ensures that the top of the 3-D model will start at the bottom of the V-Carve cut. The Rapid Z Gaps above Material settings at the bottom of the Material Setup window control the distance the bit moves above the material between cuts. Set it high enough to clear any clamps or jigs that you are using. The Home/Start Position controls where the bit comes to rest after the completion of a toolpath. It's useful when you want the spindle to move away from your project at the end of a cut. Doing so often makes it easier to change the bit and material. These settings are separate from the XY Datum and Z-Zero locations and have no effect on them. Run a couple of test files to explore how they work. Click OK to save the settings.

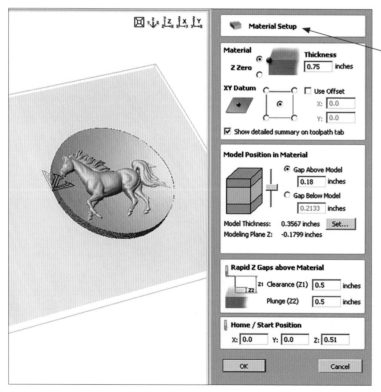

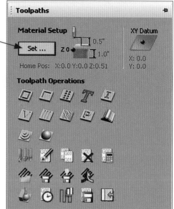

Step 11: The *Material Setup* window controls the position of the 3-D model in the material and a couple of other machine settings. Select *Gap Above Model* option and enter .18", which is the same dimension we used for the *Flat Clearance Tool* in the *V-Carve/Engraving Toolpath.* The light tan section in the middle represents the model.

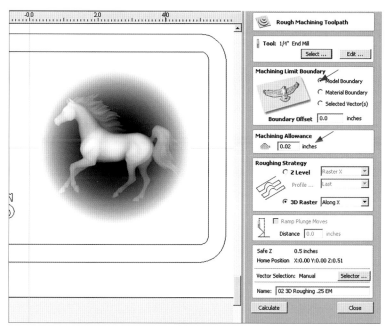

Select the clipart and click on the Rough Machining Toolpath. Select the ¼" End Mill bit, check Model Boundary, change the toolpath name, and click Calculate, **Step 12**. Selecting Model Boundary limits the rough carving to just the model. The Machining Allowance represents the minimum amount of material the roughing bit will leave behind. On larger carvings use a larger diameter bit for the roughing step. Remember you can always preview the cut, so experiment with different bit combinations.

Step 12: The *Rough Machining Toolpath* is used to remove most of the waste, making it easier for the finishing bit to do its work in the *Finish Machining Toolpath.* Using an end mill bit is the quickest way to accomplish this roughing step. Match the rest of the settings in this window, enter text in the *Name* field, and click *Calculate*.

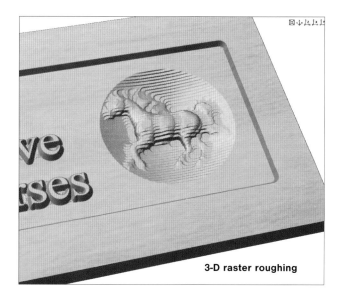

3-D raster roughing

Z-level roughing

The *3-D Raster Roughing Strategy* leaves an even amount of material on top of the 3-D shape and is a good choice when using small ¹⁄₁₆"- or ¹⁄₈"-diameter ballnose bits for the finishing pass. The *Z Level Roughing Strategy* is quicker, but leaves more material behind and is a good choice when using larger finishing bits.

Click on the Finish Machining Toolpath, **Step 13**. Select the ¼" Ballnose bit from the Tool Database, check Material Boundary, rename the toolpath, and click Calculate. If you want more detail in the carving, use a ⅛"- or ¹⁄₁₆"-diameter bit. The Stepover amount is an important setting to consider. Somewhere between 7 to 14 percent works best. A setting above 11 percent tends to leave noticeable toolpath marks, which, depending on your design, may need to be cleaned up with sanding or hand carving.

A setting of less than 7 percent increases machining time without noticeable improvement to the carving. Complete the toolpaths by adding a profile toolpath around the plaque, **Step 14**. Use Preview Toolpath to check your work. Make corrections as necessary before outputting the toolpaths. If you make changes, remember to click the Reset Preview button before previewing the toolpaths again. Also, be aware that while smaller bits provide more detail, they also increase

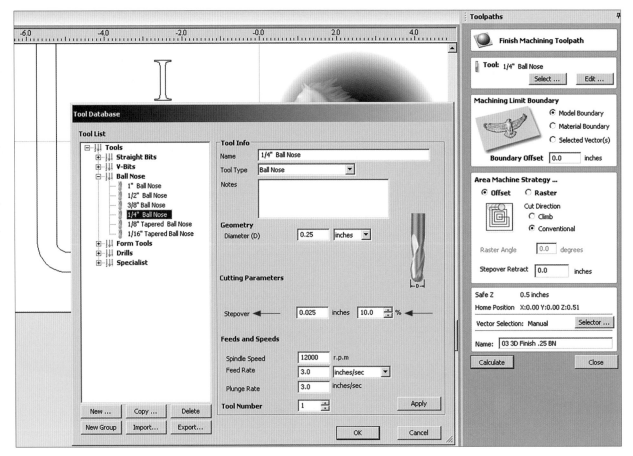

Step 13: Detail the 3-D carving using the ***Finish Machining Toolpath***. It's common to use a ¹⁄₁₆"- or ⅛"-diameter ballnose bit when carving models of this size and detail, but a ¼" ballnose is a good bit to practice with since it takes less time. Match the remaining settings and then ***Calculate*** to complete this toolpath.

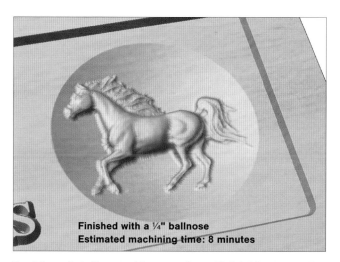

Finished with a ¼" ballnose
Estimated machining time: 8 minutes

Finished with a ¹⁄₁₆" ballnose
Estimated machining time: 28 minutes

Deciding what diameter bit to use for a *Finish Machining Toolpath* is always a compromise between machining time and carving resolution.

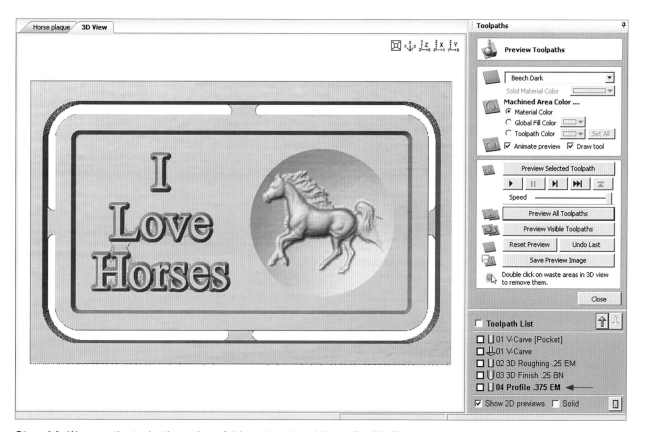

Step 14: Wrap up the toolpath portion of this project by adding a *Profile Toolpath* with *Tabs* for the perimeter cut of this plaque.

machining time. For some projects, the added detail may not be worth the added machining time.

Save each of the toolpaths the same way you did on the last project, with one exception. Because we're using a ⅜" bit for more than one cut, we can output both toolpaths together. Select the 01 V-Carve [Pocket] toolpath and the 04 Profile .375 EM toolpath. At the top of the menu check Output All Visible Toolpaths to One File. Choose your post processor and save the toolpaths. When running on the CNC machine, the two ⅜" toolpaths will automatically run one after the other. If you inadvertently select a toolpath that uses a different bit, an error message, will appear when you try to save the file, letting you know you've made a mistake.

Machining your project

Mount your material to the CNC machine, install the ⅜" bit, and run the toolpaths, **Step 15**. This will cut the profile pass, with its tabs, and clear the waste from the V-carved area. Install the 60° V-bit and make the next cut, **Step 16**. Swap to the ¼" bit and do the 3-D roughing pass, **Step 17**. Finally, use the ¼" ballnose bit to complete the 3-D finishing pass, **Step 18**. Remember that each time you change bits you must rezero the Z axis. The CNC work on your project is complete. Cut through the tabs, sand them flush, and finish sand the project.

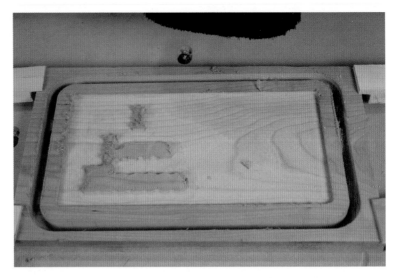

Step 15: Run the ⅜" bit toolpaths first. This will clear out the waste surrounding the text and cut the profile around the board. The tabs keep the project connected to the outer frame, which is clamped to the machine.

Step 16: Run the V-bit to detail the text.

Step 17: Run the ¼" straight bit for the 3-D roughing pass.

Step 18: The 3-D finishing pass completes the 3-D carving and is the final cut for this project.

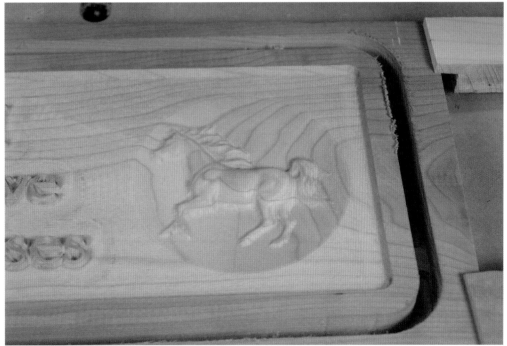

CHAPTER 8

CHAPTER 8

Practice Project 3:

Bitmap Tracing & Texture Carving

This project continues to add to what you've learned in the previous two projects. In this chapter, you'll learn how to:

- **Create vectors from a bitmap picture**
- **Create geometric designs**
- **Create textured toolpaths**
- **Machine a chamfered edge**

N

W · E

S

Lake Superior
Getchi Gumee
"Thanks for the fish."

Job Setup and design

Open a new design file and enter the Job Setup parameters, **Step 1**. This project uses the lower left for the XY Datum Position. The rectangles and offsets are created the same as they were in the previous projects, **Step 2**. Center them in the drawing during the drawing phase or afterward using the Align Objects tool.

VCarve Pro has a bitmap tracing tool that allows you to import a picture file and outline (trace) it with a vector line. This vector line can be used to create a toolpath. The first step is to import your picture, **Step 3**, and then use the Trace Bitmap tool to outline the picture with a vector, **Step 4**.

This tool can trace black and white or colored images. For this picture, we'll select the Color setting. Since it's a single-color image, we can reduce the Number of Colors to just two: blue for the image and white for the background. Next check the box(es) next to the color(s) you want to trace (Colors to Fit Vectors to). This will change

The CAD tools you'll need for this project include two new ones: the Import Bitmap for Tracing and the Draw Star tool.

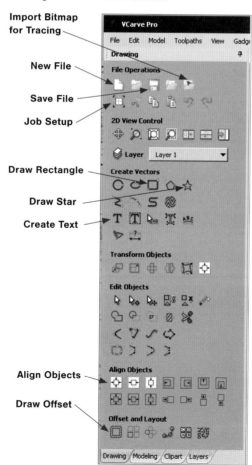

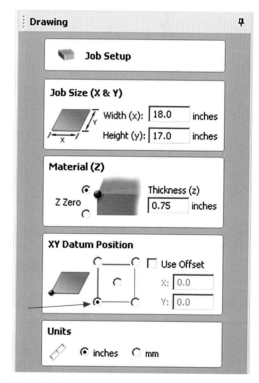

Step 1: Set up a new design file using these settings and save it to your computer. Note that the **XY Datum Position** is set to the lower left for this project.

Step 2: Use the *Draw Rectangle* tool to create the outer rectangle (centered on the material) and the *Offset Selected Vectors* tool for the two inner rectangles.

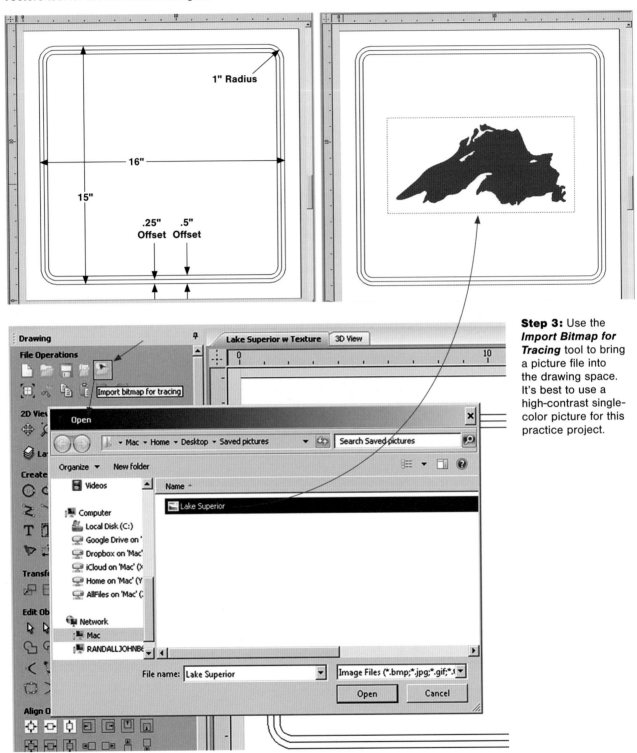

Step 3: Use the *Import Bitmap for Tracing* tool to bring a picture file into the drawing space. It's best to use a high-contrast single-color picture for this practice project.

Step 4: Open the **Trace Bitmap** tool. Match the settings here and click **Preview** to create a vector line around the selected colors. When you like the results, click **Apply** and **Close** to save.

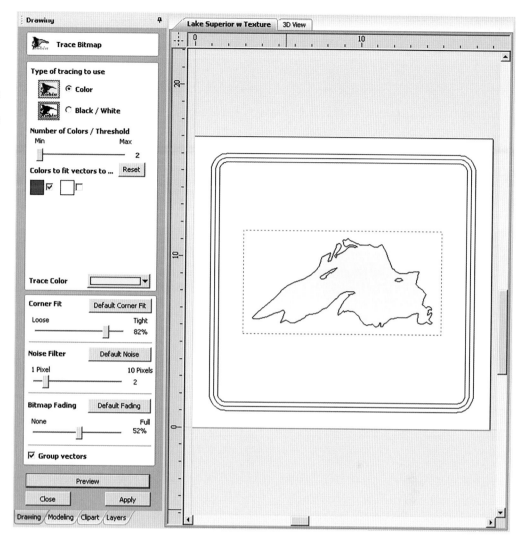

the selected colors to the Trace Color to make it easier to see what has been selected for tracing.

The Trace Bitmap tool is a powerful way to create vector lines from almost any high-contrast picture, whether it's a hand-drawn napkin sketch, piece of clipart, or a high-contrast photograph. Bitmaps such as clipart, single color images, or high-contrast photos work best for this process. Images with graduation or shading do not work as well for bitmap tracing because there is

no strong separation between the colors. Other types of software, such as Adobe Illustrator, can also be used to trace bitmap pictures to create vector drawings for use in VCarve Pro.

Layers, **Step 5**, are a powerful way to keep the parts of your drawing separated. The more complex your design becomes, the more you'll appreciate layers. If you've never used layers, think of them as sheets of transparent paper stacked on top of each other. Each layer can have its own

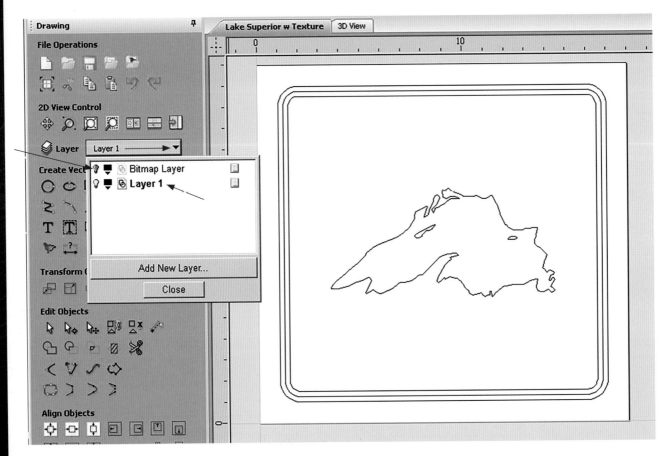

set of lines. You can choose to view them all at the same time or hide one or more to get them out of the way while working on other parts of your design. Layers work slightly different in various CAD programs, but it's always important to pay attention to which layer is "active", since new lines and edits get placed on that layer. In VCarve Pro, the layer with the bold label is the active layer, which means when you create new vector lines or objects, they are automatically placed on that layer. The tracing process sometimes creates a few stray vectors around your drawing. If you get any of these, simply select them and delete them from the drawing.

In addition to the basic circle and rectangle tools, VCarve Pro also has a couple other handy tools for drawing geometric shapes to create ovals, polygons, and stars. Each has several parameter settings for customizing the shapes. We'll use the star tool to create the four-pointed compass shape in this project, **Step 6**.

As your design develops you'll find the need to resize and move the various objects in your design. You can use the Move Object and Set Size tools that we used in Project 3, or you can manually move and resize an object by double-clicking on it and using the control handles, **Step 7**.

Step 5: Click on the *Layer* drop-down menu arrow to view the layers for this drawing. When importing a picture, a *Bitmap Layer* is automatically created for the imported image. To hide the bitmap, uncheck the lightbulb next to the *Bitmap Layer*. The vector outline remains visible because it's on *Layer 1*.

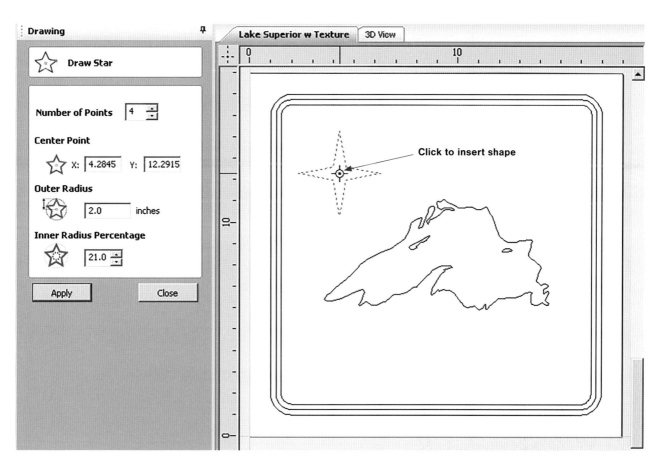

Step 6: The ***Draw Star*** tool is one of several geometric drawing tools available in VCarve Pro. You can set the exact insertion location by entering the ***Center Point*** coordinates, or simply click on the drawing to insert the shape.

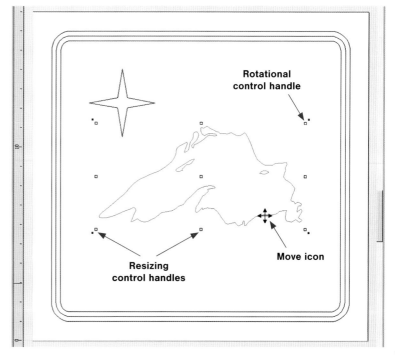

Step 7: You can manually resize or rotate a shape in VCarve Pro using the control handles. You can move it by clicking on it and dragging it to a new location. This is a quick way to roughly size and position the parts of your design.

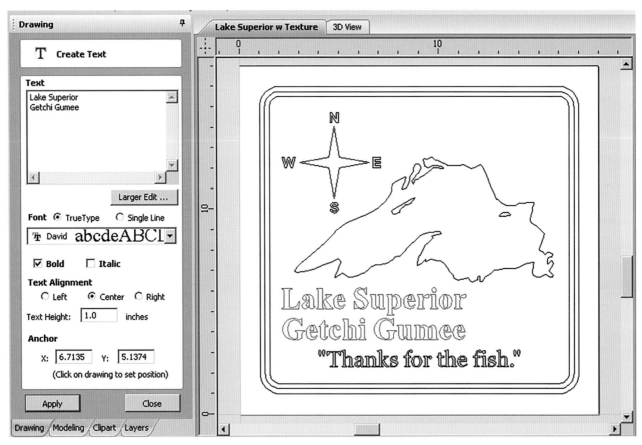

Step 8: Add text to your design. Each font style and size requires a separate setup, but this also allows them to be positioned independently of the other. The N, W, E, and S are each a separate setup, which makes it easier to locate them around the star shape.

These are the toolpath tools used in this project.

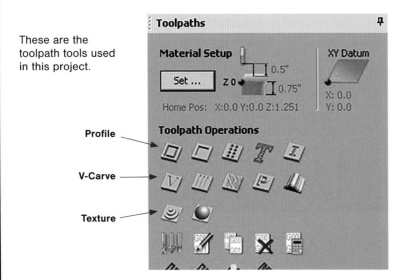

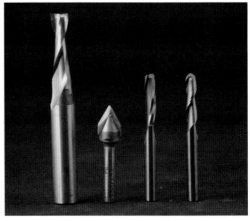

The bits we'll use for this project include a ⅜" upcut straight bit, a ½"-diameter 60° V-bit, ¼"-diameter upcut straight bit, and a ¼"diameter spiral ballnose bit.

Step 9: We're using the *V-Carve/ Engraving Toolpath* to give the edge of the lake a slight bevel, but we'll also use the *Flat Area Clearance Tool* to clear out the center of the lake. Match these settings and click *Calculate* to save.

We used text in the past two projects, so you know the basic process. For this project, we use three fonts, and each requires a separate setup, **Step 8**. Each font can be sized separately using the Create Text tool, or you could manually resize and move the font with its control handles like we saw in Step 7.

Toolpath setup and machining

The toolpath setup for this project starts with V-carving the lake shape, **Step 9**, but it's done with the addition of an end mill bit

to clear out the flat center area first. Setting a Flat Depth is necessary when V-carving shapes with large open areas. Failure to set a Flat Depth will cause the V-bit to cut all the way through the project material. However, if you forget to set it, VCarve Pro will give you a warning that you are about to cut all the way through the project, so you can go back and add it. Setting a Flat Depth is useful for design reasons too, so experiment with the option when you're setting up a V-carving. You could let the V-bit machine the entire flat bottom, but it would take a lot longer and leave a

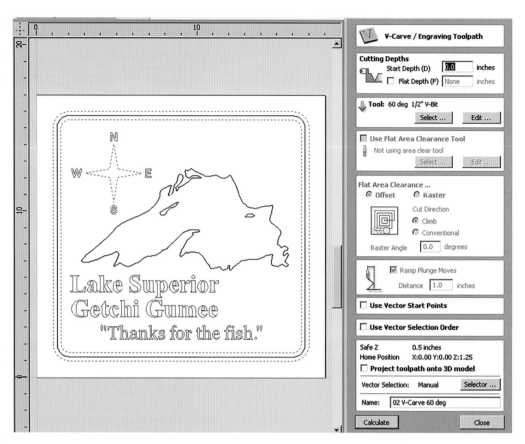

Step 10: We're using the same 60° V-bit for the text and the border but have left the *Flat Depth* unchecked. Note that we've selected just the inside and outside border rectangles. This is the first step in creating the chamfered edge on this project.

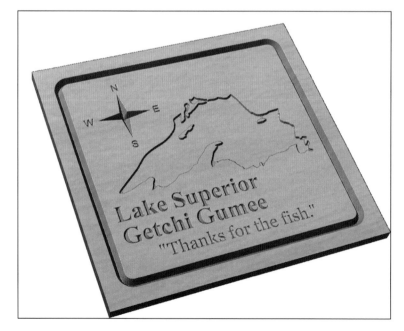

rougher surface than an end mill. So, it's more common to select the Use Flat Area Clearance Tool option. This will generate two toolpaths when you click Calculate: one using the end mill to clear the flat area and the other using the V-bit to add the bevel around the vector's perimeter. The V-bit will also flatten areas that were too small for the end mill. When you're at your machine, run the flat area clearance toolpath first.

In **Step 10**, we'll use the same V-bit in the V-Carve/Engraving Toolpath but without a Flat Depth set. This will allow the V-bit to cut to the full depth for the text, border, and star shapes. You'll notice that we've

Step 11: The *Texture Toolpath* gives you a way to add simulated hand-carved textures to your project using almost any bit. There are several *Texture Settings* that you can explore, and once you find a group of settings that you like, you can *Save* them and *Load* them into into other projects designs.

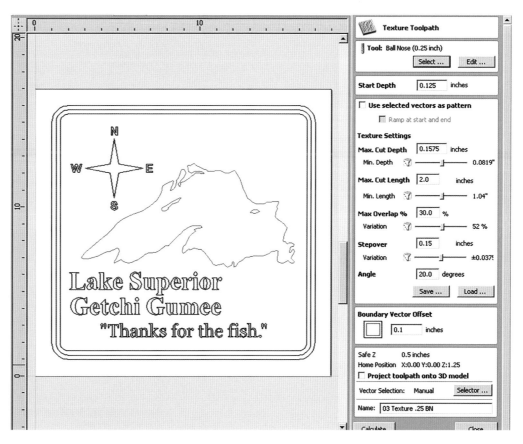

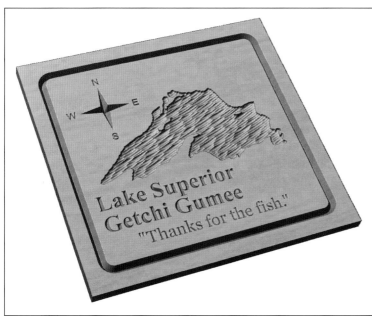

selected several different vectors at that same time. This saves time now and at your machine, but it's important to first preview the results in VCarve because adding multiple lines to a V-Carve/Engraving Toolpath can create some unexpected results. If that happens, go back to the toolpath and leave out a few shapes and Calculate it again until you get the results you desire.

The Texture Toolpath can be used to add a simulated hand-carved texture inside any closed vector shape, such as a circle, square, or this organic lake shape, **Step 11**. The Texture Toolpath is controlled by setting several parameters, including the cutting

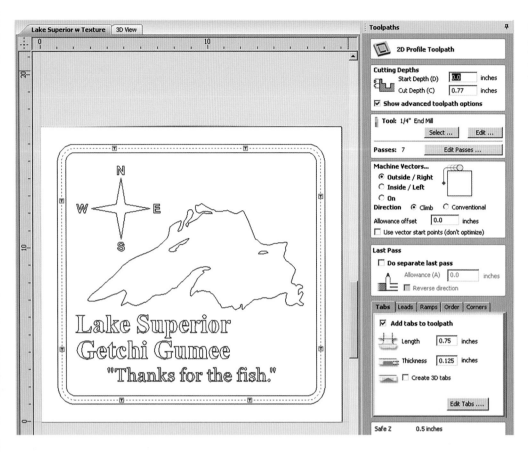

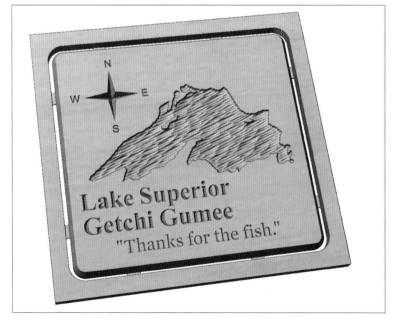

Step 12: Use the *2-D Profile Toolpath* with *Tabs* to cut out the plaque. Setting the toolpath to the outside of the middle rectangle will leave half of the V-carving, creating a chamfered edge to the plaque.

angle. For this texture, we set the angle to 20° so carving runs parallel to the NW shore of the lake shape. For texture carving, we're using a ¼" ballnose bit. We need to set the Start Depth to .125" so it matches the Pocket Toolpath depth used to recess the lake area. On this project, we're also adding a small Boundary Vector Offset to keep the texture carving tool from touching the V-carved edge of the lake.

Using the Profile Toolpath with Tabs for this project is the same as the previous projects. However, we're using it to split in half the V-carving created in Step 10. This results in chamfered edges around the plaque, **Step 12**.

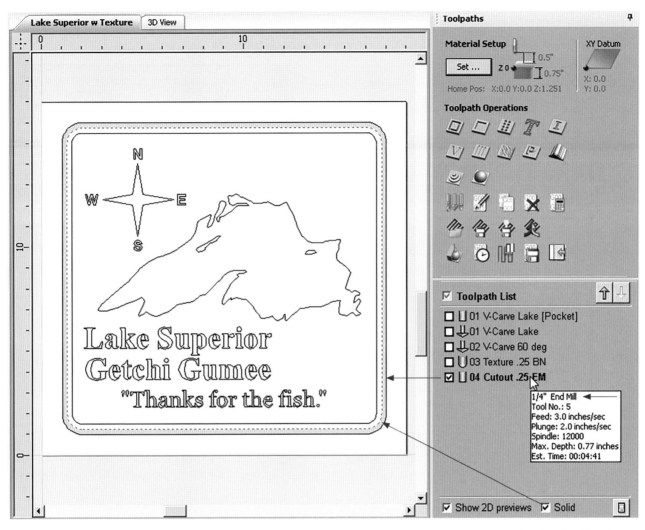

Step 13: You can preview the cutting locations of toolpaths in the 2-D window by checking the boxes next to **Solid** and the toolpath(s) you want to view. You can also view a summary of the toolpath parameters by holding the cursor over the selected toolpath. It's a quick way to check your settings without reopening the toolpath.

Using the Preview Toolpath window is a great way to verify results of the toolpaths you've created. Another useful preview tool is the Solid toolpath preview, which allows you to verify that the toolpath is cutting on the correct side of the line, **Step 13**. The toolpath(s) will appear as a light purple in the 2-D drawing.

You can also add color to the 3-D view of your design, **Step 14**. This is especially useful if you're designing a sign for someone and want to show them an illustration of how the sign will look after it's painted. A toolpath can have only one color assigned to it, so sometimes you may need to split some toolpaths that contain

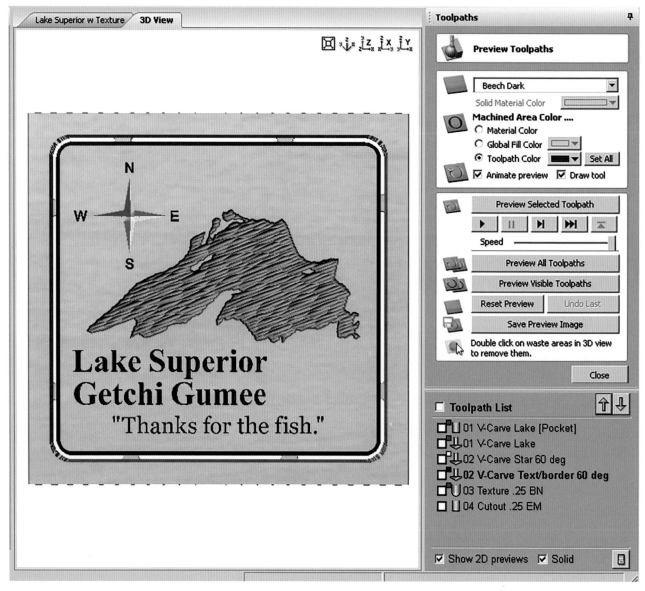

Step 14: You can add color to your design in the **Preview Toolpaths** window. First, select a toolpath (name turns bold) from the **Toolpath List,** and then add a **Toolpath Color** from the drop-down at the top of the window. The assigned color will show up next to the toolpath name.

multiple vectors into separate toolpaths to achieve your desired color layout. You can still combine these toolpaths by saving them as single cutting file during post processing.

One final quality check that you can perform in VCarve Pro is to preview the route the tool travels as it passes through and above the material, **Step 15.** This is a good way to check if the bit or spindle

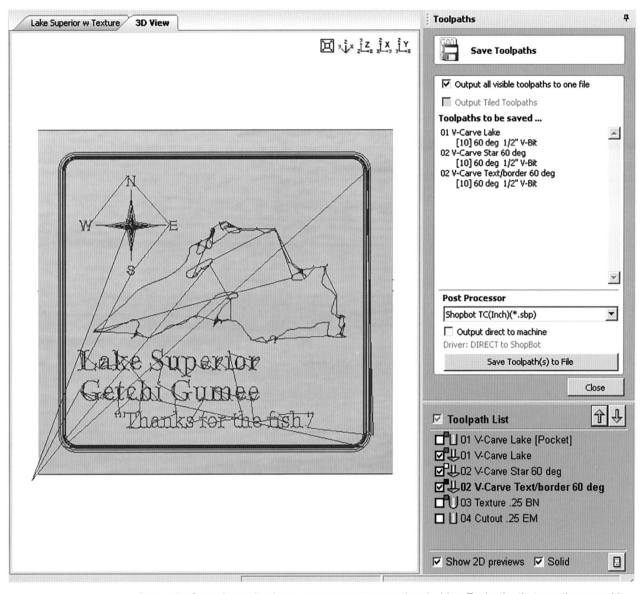

Step 15: *Save* the toolpaths to your computer or a thumb drive. Toolpaths that use the same bit (and that you want to run together) can be saved to a single cutting file. To save multiple toolpaths as a single cutting file, check the box at the top of the window and the boxes next to the toolpaths you want to combine.

will come near any hold-down clamps or devices you plan to use. The blue lines represent the bit cutting in the material, while the red lines show the bit moving over the material to the next cutting location. When you're satisfied with your design and toolpaths, save the cutting files and take them to your machine for cutting.

CHAPTER 9

Practice Project 4:

Two-Sided Machining & 3-D Texturing

This advanced project builds on skills learning in previous projects, and shows you how flip your project to machine the other side. This technique expands the types of projects you can pursue with your CNC machine. In this project, we'd create an oval box lid that is domed and textured on one face, and rabbeted to fit the box on the other. In this project, you'll learn how to:

- **Set up a two-sided project file**
- **Create an oval dome model**
- **Apply a texture to a 3-D shape**
- **Register work for two-sided machining**

Designing

Like we've done before, the first step is creating a new file, **Step 1**. The material for this project is 1" x 8" x 14". In the Job Setup window, set Z-Zero to the top of the material and the XY Datum Position to the center.

Since we'll be cutting from both faces, this project needs registration holes that allow you to machine one face, flip the board over, and accurately pin the board to the spoilboard in the same location. The holes will be drilled through the blank and slightly into the spoilboard. For this project,

we're centering them on the Y axis. For other projects, you may find centering the registration holes on the X axis is a better option. It primarily depends on where there's room to make the holes.

Click on the Draw Circle tool, **Step 2**. Create two circles with a diameter of ⅜" (type .35 in the D box), one at each end of the blank, outside of the project area. For the Center Point use 0 as the value for X, and -6 for Y. Click Create to insert a circle below the Y axis. Change the Y value to 6 and click Create again to place the next circle above the Y axis.

Top side

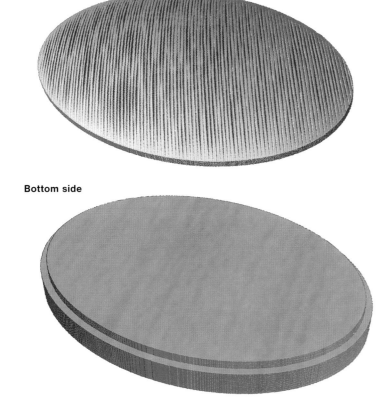

Bottom side

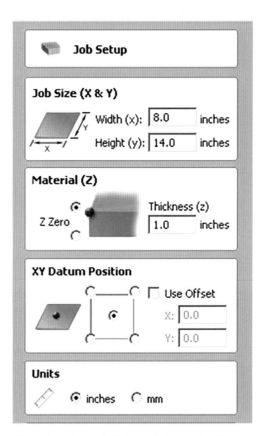

Step 1: In the *Job Setup* window, enter the *Job Size* plus the *Z-Zero* and *XY Datum Position* locations.

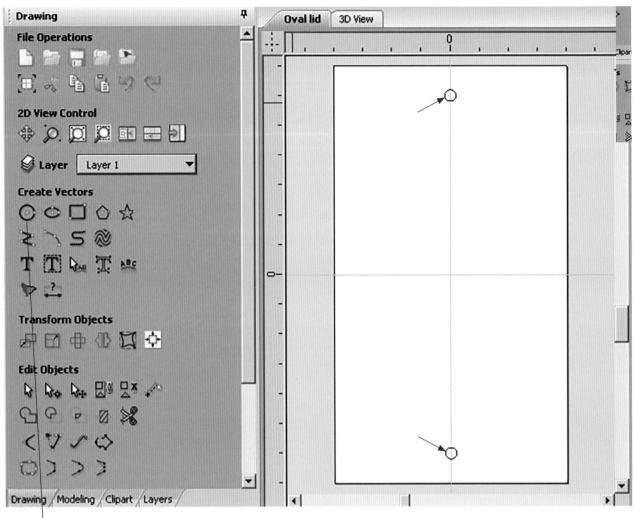

Create the dome by clicking on the Clipart tab. Once the tab opens, select Clipart, and then click Domes (Dishes). Double-click Dome_Dish 30.v3M, and it will appear on your workpiece, **Step 3**. The next step is changing the dome from a circle to an oval. Use the Set Size tool, **Step 4**. Uncheck Link XY, and adjust the X value to 6 ½" (type 6.5) and Y value to 9 ½" (type 9.5). Click Apply. The round dome changes into an oval. Note that the dimensions change slightly, on their own. This slight

Step 2: Use the *Draw Circle* tool to create and locate the registration holes required for two-sided machining. The two holes allow the project to be machined, flipped, pinned to the bed, and machined again.

Step 3: Navigate to **Domes (Dishes)** in the **Clipart** tab. Double-click on the 3-D clipart to transfer it to your drawing.

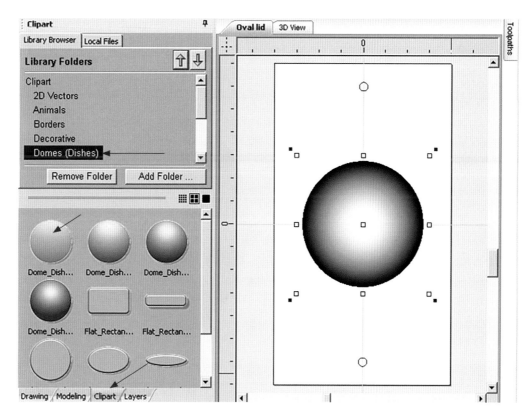

Step 4: Change the circular dome to an oval by using the **Set Size** tool. Change the **Width (X)** and **Height (Y)** values to the desired dimensions. Remember to uncheck **Link XY**. Click **Apply** and the round dome will change to an oval.

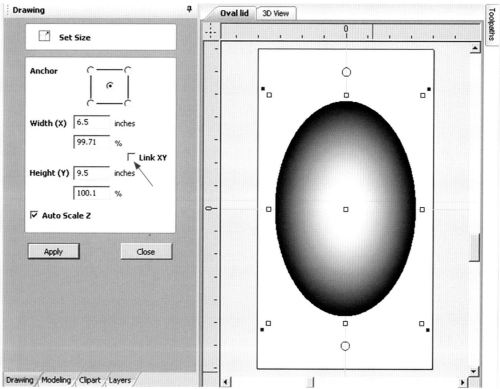

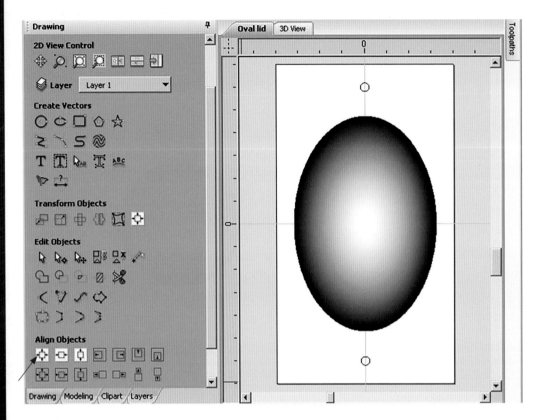

Step 5: Use the **Center in Material** alignment tool to center the oval horizontally and vertically. Centering your design on the material is an important aspect of two-sided carving, and using the **Align Objects** tools ensures that it's accurately centered.

change is simply a function of the 3-D clipart, and won't affect the final project. Use the Center in Material tool to center the dome on the workpiece, **Step 5**.

As a 3-D model, the dome is not defined by a vector, so we need to add one. Click on the Draw Ellipse tool, enter 0 for X and Y under Anchor Point, and enter the dimensions used for the dome, 6½" x 9½" (type 6.5 and 9.5), **Step 6**. Click Create to add the perimeter vector that we'll use to cut out the final shape of the dome.

A clearance cut around the dome is required to prevent the texture tool from running into the surrounding material. Create a clearance oval by using the Offset Vectors tool. Select Outwards/Right, and

set a distance of ¾" (type .75). Click Offset to create the oval, **Step 7**.

Toolpaths

This project calls for three bits. The ⅜" bit will be used to drill the registration holes. It should be an upcut spiral bit, rather than a straight fluted bit and definitely not a downcut spiral. The upcut spiral will act like a drill bit, removing chips from the cut. Be sure the cut length is 1.25" or more, so it's long enough to drill all the way through the material and into the spoilboard. An upcut spiral bit pulls up on the material, so be sure the material is securely held down.

Before creating your toolpaths, locate the dome within the thickness of the

Step 6: The *Draw Ellipse* tool is used to create an oval around the dome. The oval is necessary to create a vector for the toolpath to follow.

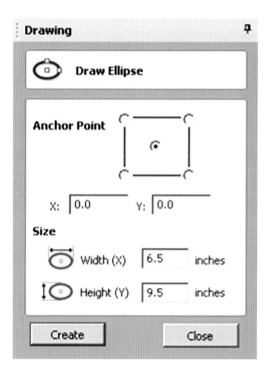

Step 7: Use the *Offset Vectors* tool to create a larger oval offset by ¾" (type .75). This oval will be used to create the clearance area for the texture tool.

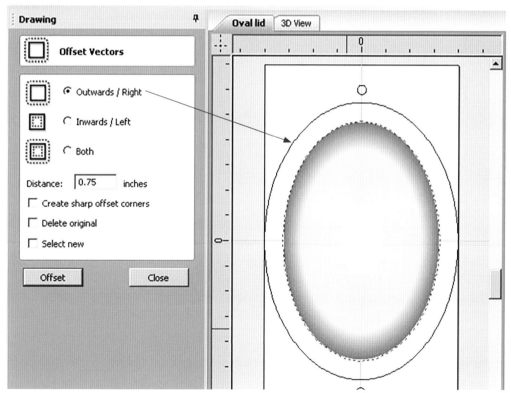

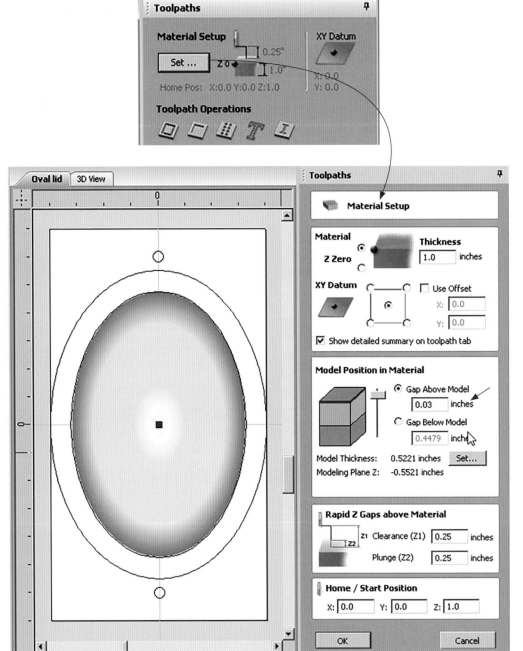

Step 8: In the *Material Setup* window, set the 3-D model slightly below the surface of your material. It's important to correctly locate the dome in the material so that we can machine both faces.

material, **Step 8.** Set the Model Position in the Material Setup window so the Gap Above Model is .03". Click OK. Positioning the dome at this location provides a slight amount of cutting waste above the dome,

and leaves enough material to cut the lip on the bottom side of the lid.

Create the toolpath for the registration holes by using the Drilling Toolpath, **Step 9.** Within the Drilling Toolpath menu, select

Step 9: Use *Drilling Toolpath* to bore the two registration holes. Select both registration holes by clicking on one, then hold the **Shift** key and clicking on the second hole. This selection technique is useful whenever you need to select multiple objects.

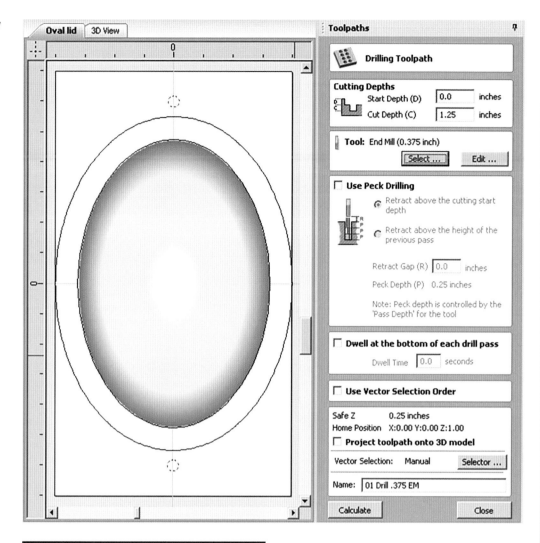

This project uses three bits: ⅜"-diameter upcut spiral, ½"-diameter core box, and a 60° V-bit.

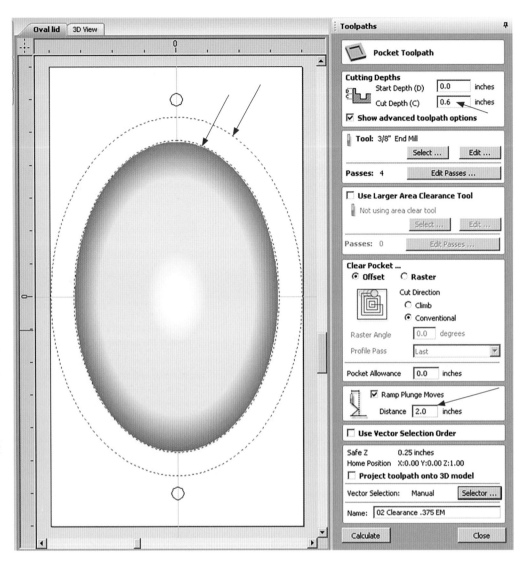

Step 10: Use the **Pocket Toolpath** to create the clearance cut around the dome. It's important to select both oval vectors for this toolpath. Set the **Cut Depth** and enter 2" for **Ramp Plunge Moves**.

the ⅜" End Mill bit, set depth for 1.25", rename the toolpath, and click Calculate. You'll get a message warning you that the toolpath exceeds the material thickness. Click OK.

The clearance oval is created using the Pocket Toolpath, **Step 10**. Set Cut Depth (C) to .6", select the ⅜" End Mill bit, and for the Clear Pocket select Offset and Conventional. Check the Ramp Plunge

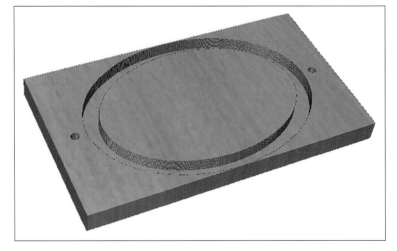

Step 11: Set up a *Rough Machining Toolpath* to remove the waste from the dome.

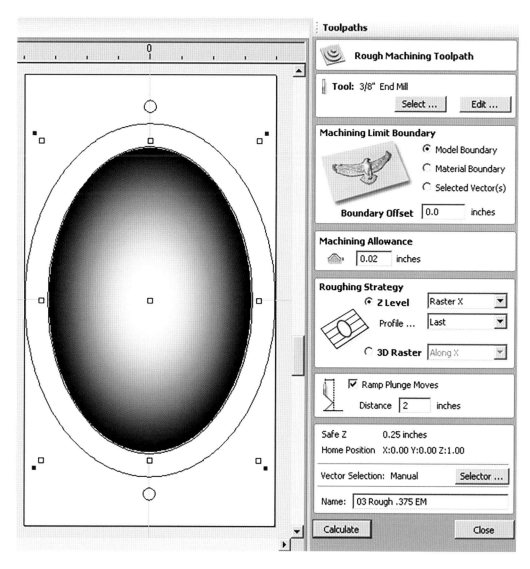

Toolpaths

🌀 **Rough Machining Toolpath**

Tool: 3/8" End Mill

[Select ...]   [Edit ...]

Machining Limit Boundary
- ⦿ Model Boundary
- ○ Material Boundary
- ○ Selected Vector(s)

Boundary Offset `0.0` inches

Machining Allowance
`0.02` inches

Roughing Strategy
- ⦿ **Z Level** `Raster X ▼`
  - Profile ... `Last ▼`
- ○ **3D Raster** `Along X ▼`

☑ Ramp Plunge Moves
Distance `2` inches

Safe Z   0.25 inches
Home Position   X:0.00 Y:0.00 Z:1.00

Vector Selection: Manual   [Selector ...]

Name: `03 Rough .375 EM`

[Calculate]   [Close]

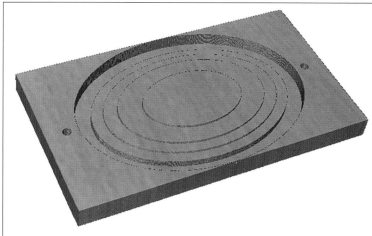

Moves and set the Distance to 2". Rename the toolpath and click Calculate.

Select the dome and start shaping it by using the Rough Machining Toolpath, **Step 11**. Select the ⅜" bit, set the Machining Limit Boundary as Model Boundary, rename the toolpath, and click Calculate. Do the final shaping with a Finish Machining Toolpath, **Step 12**. Select the ½" Ballnose bit, Model Boundary, name the toolpath, and click Calculate.

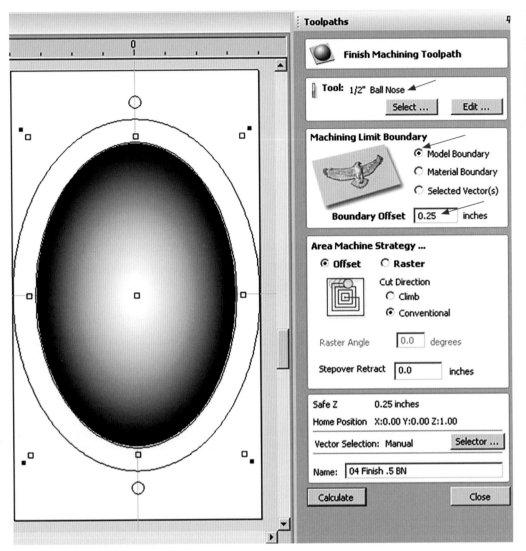

Step 12: Finalize the dome shape using the **Finish Machining Toolpath** and a ½" ballnose. Select **Model Boundary** to restrict the carving to just the surface of the model.

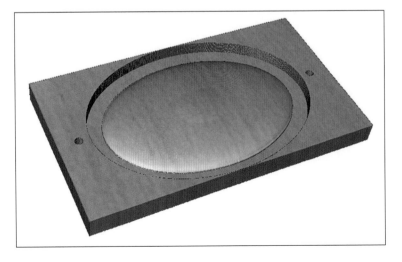

Step 13: Adding texture to objects makes wonderful use of a CNC machine's capabilities. Various textures are possible by just changing the texture settings and using different router bits.

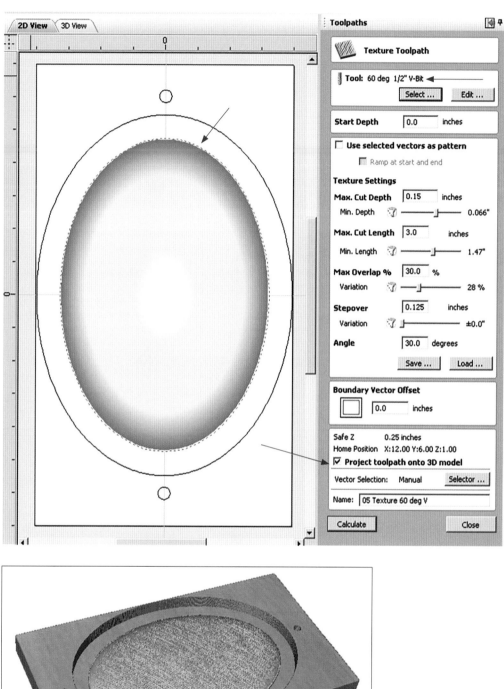

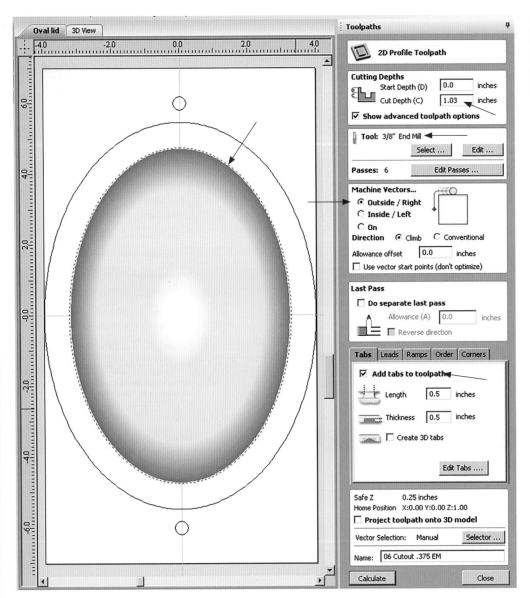

Step 14: To cut out the lid use a ***Profile Toolpath***. Set the ***Cut Depth*** to slightly more than the material thickness. Check ***Add Tabs to Toolpath***.

Add texture to the dome by selecting both the dome model and the oval vector outline that defines it, **Step 13**. Open the Texture Toolpath window and match all the settings. There are several settings in this window and it's fun to experiment with these various settings. Be sure to check the box next to Project Toolpath onto 3-D Model. Checking this box applies the texture onto the contour of the 3-D dome. Name the toolpath and click Calculate.

Step 15: Open the *Toolpath Tabs* window to edit the tabs. Remember that you can click on a tab to remove it, or click on the toolpath to add one. Four tabs are sufficient.

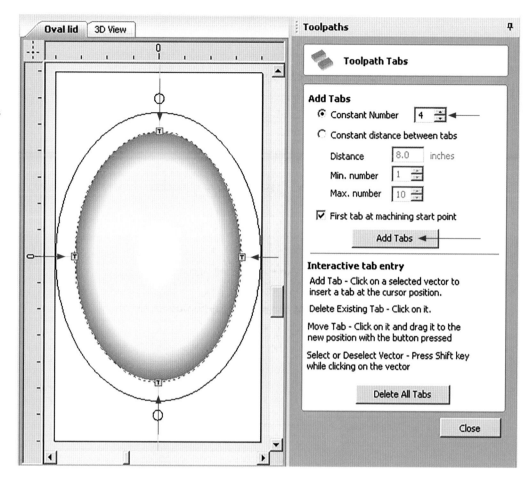

Select the oval surrounding the dome and use the Profile Toolpath to cut it, **Step 14**. Set the Cut Depth to 1.03", and select the ⅜" bit. Be sure the Machine Vectors are set up to cut Outside/Right. Under Tabs, check

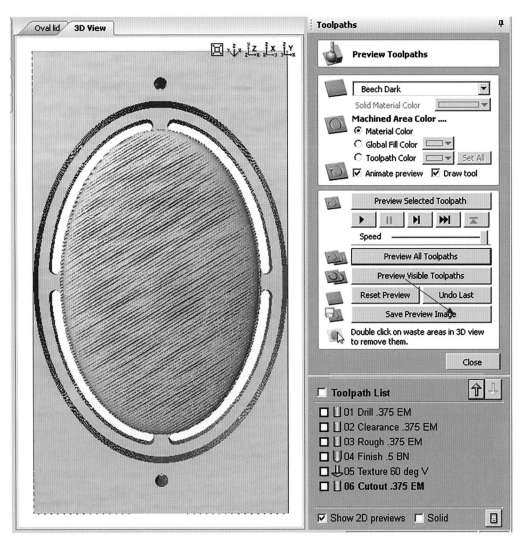

Step 16: It's fun to see your project appear when you use the *Preview Toolpaths* function. And, this will help you find errors in the design and toolpaths.

Add Tabs to Toolpath. Because we're cutting from both faces, we need to make the tabs thicker than normal. Set the tab Thickness to ½". Click Edit Tabs, **Step 15**. Four tabs are sufficient. Click Add Tabs, name the toolpath, and click Calculate.

Check your work by using the Preview Toolpaths function, **Step 16**. The Preview provides an opportunity to double-check the design and toolpaths. If you make changes, click Reset Preview to erase the current view, and then click Preview Toolpaths again.

Save your toolpaths. Consolidate the four cuts that use a ⅜" bit by outputting them all to one toolpath.

Step 17: Before closing this file, select and copy the oval that defines the dome.

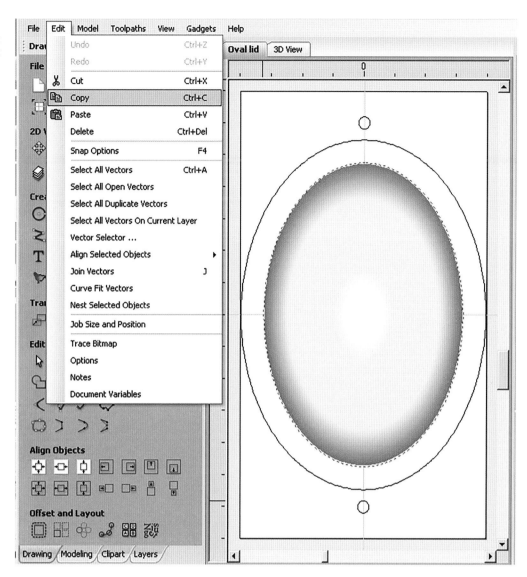

Design the back

We'll create a new file to design and create toolpaths for the back of this project. Before saving and closing the existing file, select the oval that defines the dome and copy it, **Step 17**. The Copy command can be found under Edit, or use the keyboard shortcut Control+C. Save this file and open a new one. Use the same material dimensions and zero locations we used for the first design.

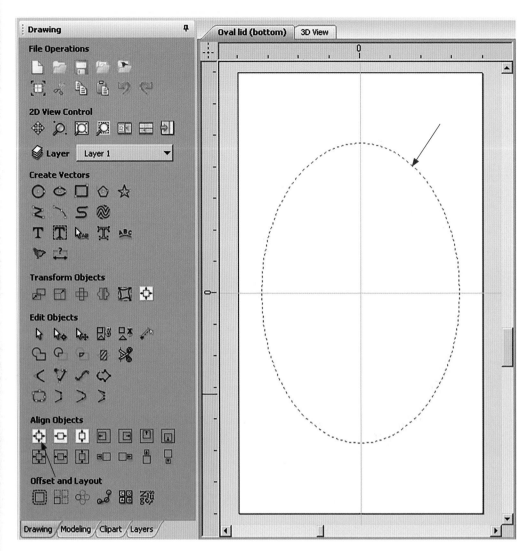

Step 18: Paste the oval into the new workspace, and center it using the *Align Objects* tool *Center in Material*.

Navigate to the Paste command under Edit, and paste the oval into the new workspace. Use the Center in Material tool to make sure the oval is perfectly centered, **Step 18**. Use the Offset Vectors tool to create a smaller oval, **Step 19**. Offset Inwards/ Left by a distance of ¼". Click Offset. This offset equals the wall thickness of the box that goes with this lid. We don't show how to make the box in this chapter, but you should now have enough CNC design skills to create a box to match this lid.

Step 19: Use the *Offset Vectors* tool to create a second inner oval. Offset it .25" *Inwards/Left* from the outer oval.

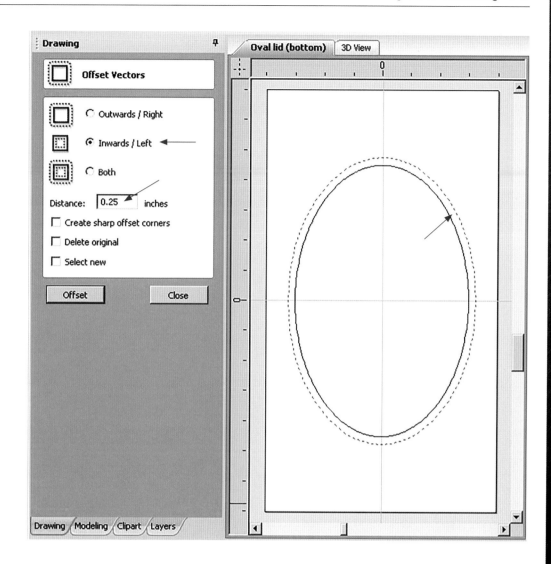

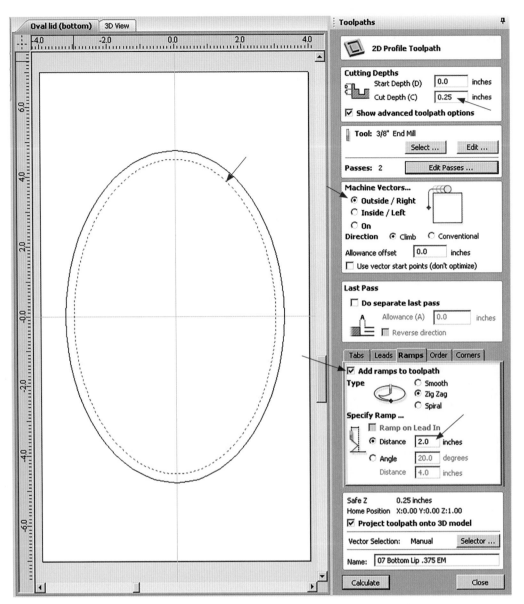

Step 20: Create a *Profile Toolpath* for the rabbet on the bottom of the lid. Set it up so it cuts .25" deep and to the *Outside/Right* of the inner oval.

Select the inner oval and open the Profile Toolpath, **Step 20**. Set a Cut Depth of ¼", and select the ⅜" bit. Under the Machine Vectors section, use Outside/Right.

Click the Ramps tab, check Add Ramps to Toolpath, and enter a Distance of 2". Name the file and click Calculate. Save the toolpath file and take it to your machine.

Machining the project

Secure the material to the CNC. We'll be cutting all the way through the piece, so be sure you have a spoilboard under your work. Install the ⅜" bit and zero the X, Y, and Z axes. Run the ⅜" bit toolpaths, **Step 21**. This cutting file includes four toolpaths.

The order of the toolpaths may matter for some projects, so organize them in VCarve Pro before post-processing them as a single saved cutting file.

Change to the ½" ball router bit to cut the 3-D finishing for the dome, **Step 22**. Install the V-bit, and run the Texturing Toolpath,

Step 21: The benefit of combining toolpaths (that use the same bit) into one cutting file is that the CNC will automatically go from one cut to the next. The cuts show here were done with just one cutting file, but it contained four toolpaths; one for drilling the registration holes, one for 3-D rough cutting the dome, one for cutting the profile with tabs, and one for creating the clearance cut around the dome. This setup is a real time saver.

Step 22: The project starts to take shape once you've run the *Finish Machining Toolpath* on the dome.

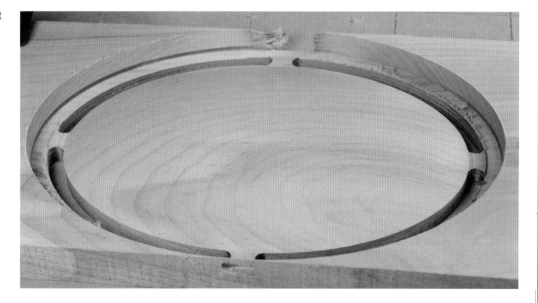

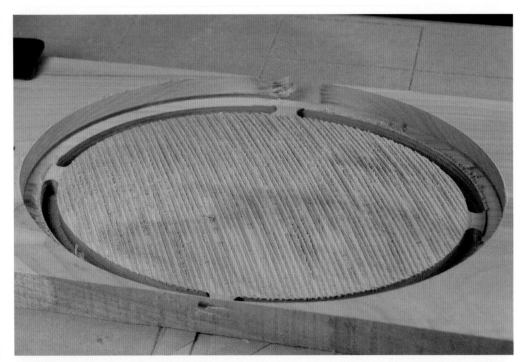

Step 23: A variety of textures can be achieved depending on what bit you use, and how you set the *Texturing Toolpath.*

Step 24: The final cut produces a rabbet on the bottom of the lid.

Step 25: Two-sided machining opens doors to many interesting CNC applications.

Step 23. Each time you change bits, remember to zero the Z axis to the top surface of the material.

The top of the lid is now complete, and we're ready to machine the rabbet on the bottom side. Flip the workpiece over. Insert ⅜" dowels through the registration holes and into the holes in the machine bed. **Step 24**. The dowels are for registration only. You must still secure the workpiece to the table. Install the ⅜" bit and zero the Z axis. Thanks to the registration pins, there's no need to zero the XY axes, and it would be a mistake to change those settings now. Run the toolpath. The CNC work on the project is complete, **Step 25**. Cut through the tabs, sand them flush, and finish-sand the project.

CHAPTER

10

Gallery

Now that you know the ins and outs of designing CNC projects, creating toolpaths, and setting up your CNC router, you're no doubt excited to get some projects going on your machine. Check out the amazing work shown here for motivation and inspiration. You're sure to find an idea (or two or three) that you like and will want to duplicate.

Furniture

Whether you're making 1 piece or 100, prototyping or crafting the final version, a CNC machine can simplify the furniture making process.

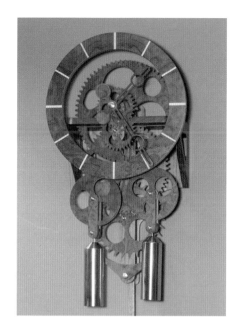

Games, Toys, and Models

Precision parts, repetitive hole locations, and contoured surfaces are common to these items, and are tasks at which CNCs excel.

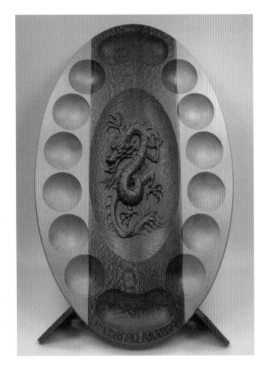

Unique Gift Items

Looking for something special for that hard-to-buy-for person in your life? A CNC machine offers a variety of gift options.

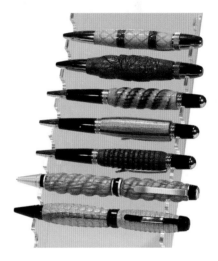

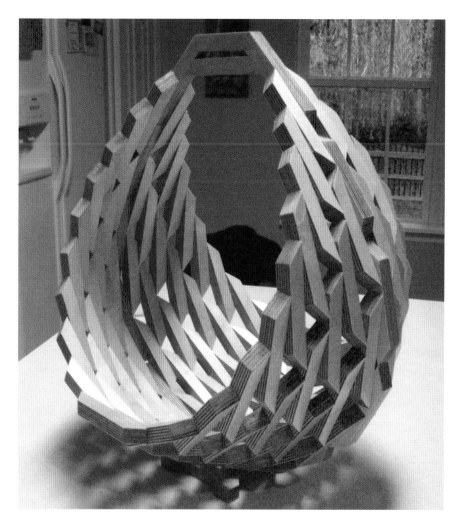

Signs and 3-D Work

One of the most common uses of a CNC machine, the sky is the limit when it comes to making custom signs and doing 3-D carving.

Index

About the Author

Randy Johnson started woodworking in his dad's shop, along with metalworking, machine tinkering, and all those things kids did before computers. His mother, a lifelong teacher, gave him a deep appreciation for learning and the arts. Those experiences put Randy on a lifelong journey that has crisscrossed between the practical and the creative. Along the way, he has managed large and small shops, served as Editor-in-Chief at *American Woodworker* magazine, and even taught woodworking in the U.S. Virgin Islands. For the past several years he's been exploring CNC router technology and ways to apply it to his woodworking. Randy lives with his wife in Minnesota, where he enjoys catamaran sailing in the summer, cross-country skiing in the winter, and woodworking all year round.

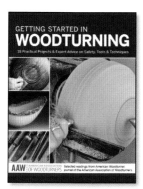
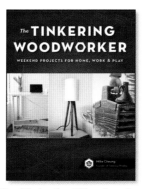

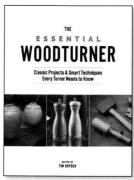

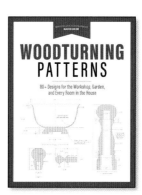

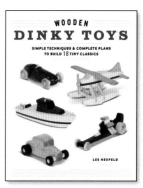

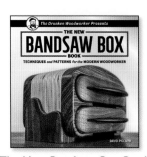

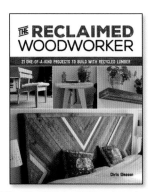

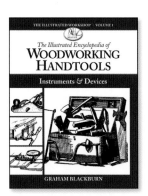
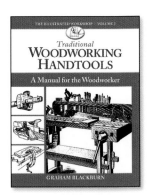

TRUMPET/CORNET

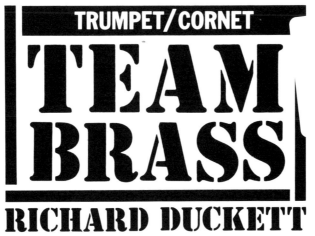

TEAM BRASS

RICHARD DUCKETT

The author is donating a percentage of his royalties from Team Brass
to a children's charity.

International Music Publications Limited

Introduction

The TEAM BRASS series has been designed to meet the needs of young brass musicians everywhere, whether lessons are given individually, in groups or in the classroom.

Musical variety

Each book contains a wide range of musical styles, from the Baroque and Classical eras to film, folk, jazz and latin American. In addition there are original pieces and studies, technical exercises and scales, progressing from the beginner stage to approximately Grade IV standard of the *Associated Board of the Royal Schools of Music*. Furthermore TEAM BRASS offers material suitable for mixed brass ensemble as well as solos with piano accompaniment.

Ensemble pieces

All TEAM BRASS books contain corresponding pages of music which can be played together in harmony. Beginners are thus given early ensemble experience and the opportunity to share sessions with other players, be they treble or bass clef, B flat, E flat or F pitched instruments, and occasionally with guitar or synthesizer.

Study options

The TEAM BRASS series is not a "method". It is a collection of primer music from which the teacher can select a suitably graded course for each pupil. This allows for variation in starting-point, concentration threshold and tempo of progression. There is in TEAM BRASS a choice of starting-notes and several choices of progressive path the pupil can follow. Study options appear at the foot of most pages.

The terms *crotchet, quaver, minim etc.*, are used throughout this series instead of *quarter-note, eighth-note, half-note etc.* It is felt that, as pupils will probably need to know both systems, the less easily remembered terms should be learned first — one at a time. Later there will be no difficulty in learning the alternative, more logically-based fraction names.

This series is ideal for use with the upper primary and lower secondary age-range.

G.C.S.E. skills

In addition to fostering musical literacy, *Rhythm Grids, Letter-name Grids,* and *Play By Ear* lines provide early opportunities for composition and improvisation. This aspect of TEAM BRASS can be a useful starting-point for these elements in the GCSE Examination course now followed in many secondary schools.

Comprehensive notes on the use of this series, scores of ensemble pieces, piano accompaniments and approaches to creative music-making are given in the *Accompaniments Book*.

Team Brass Ensemble

TEAM BRASS ensemble material has been specially written so that it can be played by almost any combination of brass instruments that the teacher is likely to encounter. The pieces are basically for duet, to which can be added independent (and inessential) third and fourth parts if required.

This book contains 11 pages of trumpet ensemble material. Related second and third parts appear in the *F Horn Book*. Also, third and fourth parts appear in the *Supplement* to the *Brass Band Book*, and fourth parts in the *Trombone/Euphonium (bass clef) Book*. Relevant parts to the trumpet ensemble appear on the same numbered page in each book, i.e., third and fourth parts to *Canzonetta* (trumpet duet) are on page 15 in all books.

The third part can be played as an effective bass line with the trumpet duets in the absence of a fourth-part player.

Second and third parts can also be used as the harmonic accompaniment for the trombone/euphonium melody. For example, on page 14 a second-part trumpet player (or hornist) and a third-part horn player can accompany a trombonist playing the melody line of *German Tune*. This ensures that the lower brass players get an opportunity to play the tune. It also means that, for performance purposes, many of the ensemble pieces extend into longer and more elaborate items with various changes of texture.

Whilst horn players (F and E flat) do not have the tune within the B flat arrangements, the *F Horn Book* has 9 pages of its own ensemble material which can be extended harmonically by using lower parts in the *Trombone/Euphonium Book*. The *Brass Band Book* also has 9 pages of ensemble which can be played in extended harmony in either B flat or E flat form.

All the ensemble pieces are graded to match the lesson material. These may be easily located by following the direction at the foot of the appropriate lesson page. Scores for all ensemble material and more extensive notes appear in the *Accompaniments Book*.

The following symbols have been used to provide an immediate visual identification:

 Pieces with Piano Accompaniment

 Part of an Ensemble arrangement (score included in *Accompaniments Book*)

Because the ensemble pieces provide a meeting point for players who are at various stages of development, these may include technical elements (new notes, rhythms etc.,) which are not in fact introduced until some pages later.

For MARY

Edited by WILLIAM RUMFORD Instrumental Organiser
for the London Borough of Brent
PHILIP EVRY and GEOFFRY RUSSELL-SMITH

Piano accompaniments by GEOFFRY RUSSELL-SMITH

INTERNATIONAL MUSIC PUBLICATIONS would like to thank the
following publishers for permission to use arrangements
of their copyright material in TEAM BRASS.
CHAPPELL MUSIC LTD. London W1Y 3FA
for LITTLE DONKEY
© 1959 Chappell Music Ltd.
WARNER BROS MUSIC LTD. London W1P 3DD
for BLOWIN' IN THE WIND
© 1962 (unpub.) © 1963 M Witmark & Sons, USA
and for STAR WARS (Main Title)
© 1977 Fox Fanfare Music Inc. USA
WILLIAMSON MUSIC LTD. London W1Y 3FA
for MY FAVORITE THINGS and EDELWEISS
© 1959 Richard Rodgers & Oscar Hammerstein II
Williamson Music Inc. USA

Sincere thanks are extended
to the following people whose criticism, advice
and help in various ways has been invaluable.
KEITH ALLEN, Senior Instrumental Teacher
for the City of Birmingham.
COLIN MOORE, County Instrumental Organiser
for East Sussex.
BRIAN WICKS, Senior Lecturer at Newman and Westhill
Colleges of Higher Education.
KEITH WATTS, Head of Brass for Sandwell Education Authority.
PETER SMALLEY, Cornet / trumpet player
and Instrumental Teacher, County of Staffordshire.
MOLLY WICKS and PHILIP LEAH, whose enthusiasm
and support have been a great encouragement.

First Published 1988

© International Music Publications Limited,
Griffin House, 161 Hammersmith Road,
London W6 8BS, England.

Book Design: Eleanor Gamper
Cover Design: Ian Barrett / Peter White
Cover Photography: Ron Goldby
Production: Peter White / Philip Evry
Reprographics: Positive Colour Ltd.
Instruments photographed by courtesy
of Vincent Bach International Ltd.

TEAM BRASS: Trumpet / Cornet
ISBN 1 84328 436 7 / Order Ref: 16695 / 215-2-429

Lesson diary & practice chart

Date (week commencing)	Enter number of minutes practised.							Teacher indicates which pages to study.
	Mon	Tue	Wed	Thur	Fri	Sat	Sun	

Getting started

Teachers, who like pupils to experiment with the instrument before learning to use the text, can write helpful notes below, according to the needs of the student.*

Otherwise proceed as follows:
Starting Note G on page 2, or
Starting Note C on page 4, or
Group Chords on page 19, or
Five-Note Patterns on page 11.

*

Lip, jaw and throat positions:

Buzzing with the lips:

Buzzing on the mouthpiece:

Long notes:

Tongued notes:

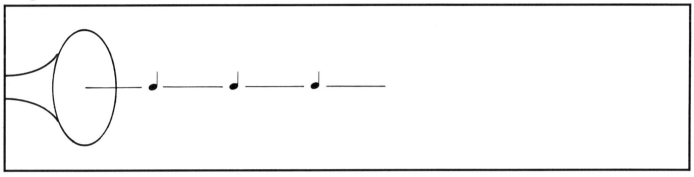

Slurring:

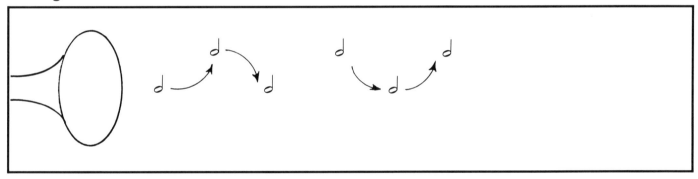

Making up rhythms and melodies, and soundscapes:

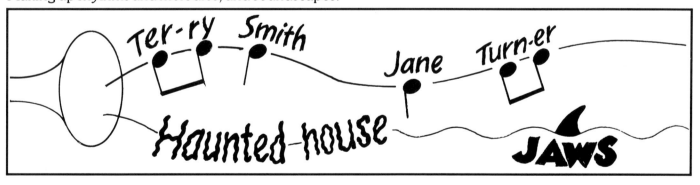

All these notes are *possible* on your instrument without using valves, by merely varying the lip-pressure. At first you will probably only be able to produce the lowest notes.

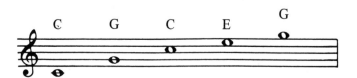

. . . then on to F

1st valve

Play the grid across, up or down

BAR LINES divide a line of notes into sets. In $\frac{4}{4}$ time each bar adds up to four crotchet beats

(2 + 1+1 = 4)   (1+1+1+1=4)

The DOUBLE BAR marks the end of a piece of music

TONGUE "tu" & "ta"

F's and G's

■ Fits with page 5, line 4.

Pavane

Slowly and sadly

■ Proceed down to E, page 6; or up to A, page 17.

or start with C . . .

. . . then on to D

1st & 3rd valves

Play the grid across, up, or down

BAR LINES divide a line of notes into sets. In 4/4 time each bar adds up to four crotchet beats

(2 + 1+1 =4)   (1+1+1+1=4)

The DOUBLE BAR marks the end of a piece of music

■ Fits with *F Book* page 3, line 3.   ## C's and D's

■ Fits with *F Book* page 3, line 4.

Fits with page 3, line 5.   ## Elegy

Slowly and sadly

■ Proceed up to E, on page 7; or down to B, on page 10.

6

The note E

1st & 2nd valves

■ This page fits harmonically & rhythmically with the one opposite

G, F and E together

PLEASE PRACTISE EVERYDAY – 20 MINS

A SEMIBREVE lasts for FOUR beats

■ Fits with page 10, line 2; with *F Book* page 1, line 8.

The lost note

19/05/06

All mixed up!

■ This can be played in conjunction with *Acapulco Bay* opposite.

Acapulco Bay

Tempo di Beguine

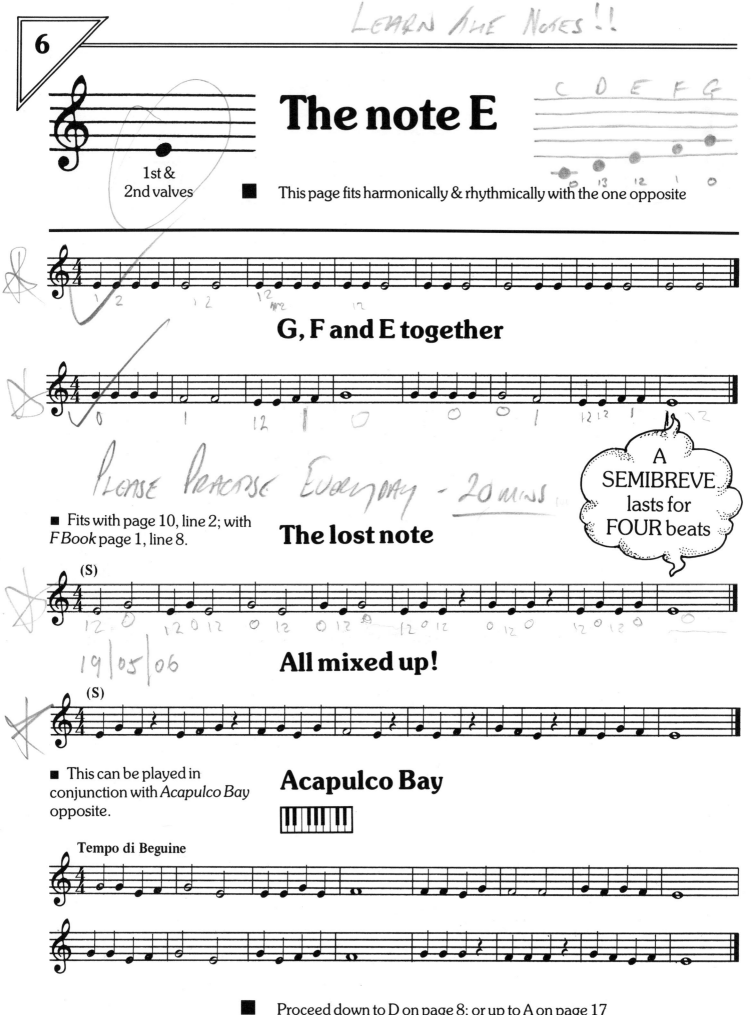

■ Proceed down to D on page 8; or up to A on page 17

The 'S' symbol means the music can be slurred throughout, if the teacher wishes.

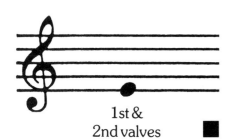

1st &
2nd valves ■ This page fits harmonically & rhythmically with the one opposite.

C, D and E together

■ When played in conjunction with *The Lost Note* (opposite) fits with *F Book*, page 1, line 8.

The lost note

A SEMIBREVE lasts for FOUR beats

Tricky tune!

■ This can be played in conjunction with *Acapulco Bay* opposite.

Acapulco Bay

Tempo di Beguine

■ Proceed up to F on page 9; or down to B on page 10.

The 'S' symbol means the music can be slurred throughout, if the teacher wishes.

G, F, E and D together

G	F	E	D	E	G	D	F	E

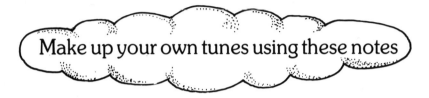

Make up your own tunes using these notes

■ If required, *see preparatory 'D' exercises on page 5.*

D
(1st and 3rd valves)

■ Fits with page 10, line 4.

Marching

■ Fits with page 10, line 5.   ## Gliding

Vigorous March   ## Watch your step!

■ *Watch your step!* can be played in conjunction with *Sort 'em out!*
(opposite), or with piano accompaniment.

C, D, E and F together

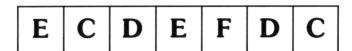

Make up your own tunes using these notes

■ If required, see *preparatory 'F' exercises on page 3.*

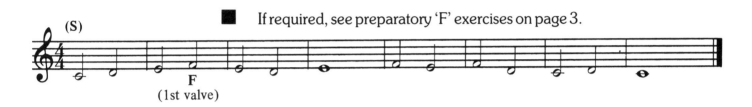

Flowing

Two bar phrase (1) | Two bar phrase (2) | Two bar phrase (3) | Two bar phrase (4)

Walking

Composed by eleven-year old JENNY WONG

Sort 'em out!

March

■ *Sort 'em out!* can be played in conjunction with *Watch your step!* (opposite).

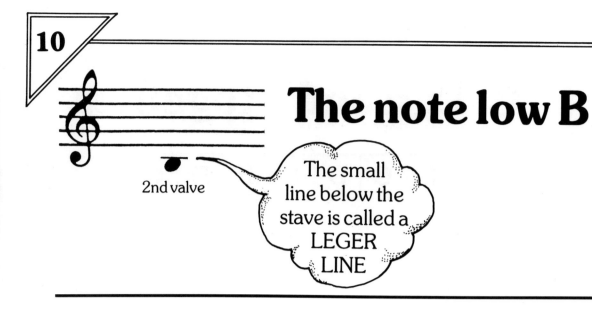

The note low B

The small line below the stave is called a **LEGER LINE**

2nd valve

■ All the material on this page integrates with material on previous pages, as marked.

■ Fits with page 2, line 5; with *F Book*, page 4, line 5.

■ Fits with page 6, line 3; with *F Book*, page 1, line 8.

■ Fits with page 6, line 4.

■ Fits with page 8, line 2.

B with C, D and E

■ Fits with page 8, line 4.

■ For related ensemble material see pages 14, 15, 19, 20, 21.

Five-note patterns

Intervals

Step round

Welsh tune

Traditional

New Rhythm

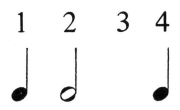

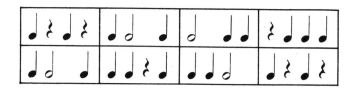

Two rounds

'C' means Common Time i.e. $\frac{4}{4}$ time

Old Liza Jane

■ Related group 'warm up' on page 19; related ensemble on pages 14 & 15; syncopated ensemble on page 21.

3/4 time

Slow waltz

Composed by
eleven-year old JOANNE AHMED

Every bar adds up to three crotchets

This means 'rest' for 4 whole bars- so count ①23 ②23 ③23 ④23 and then play from bar 5

A dotted minim lasts for THREE beats

Four bar question phrase, A

Four bar answer phrase, B

Les ballons

Gently and dreamily

getting slower

(muted, if possible)

Round lullaby

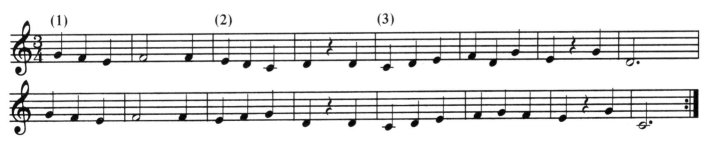

■ Proceed up to A, page 17; or to quavers, page 22; or F♯, page 24; or low A, page 36.

German tune

Duet

Traditional

Lullaby

Duet

COUNT
① 2 3 ② 2 3

■ Second and third parts to trumpet duets appear in the *F horn book*
and the supplement to the brass band book (treble clef). Fourth
parts are in *trombone book* and *supplement*.

Tied notes

A minim tied to a crotchet lasts for 3 beats.

A crotchet tied to a crotchet lasts for 2 beats.

A semibreve tied to a crotchet lasts for 5 beats and so on.

Don't be late!

Canzonetta

Compose a part for tambour or tambourine

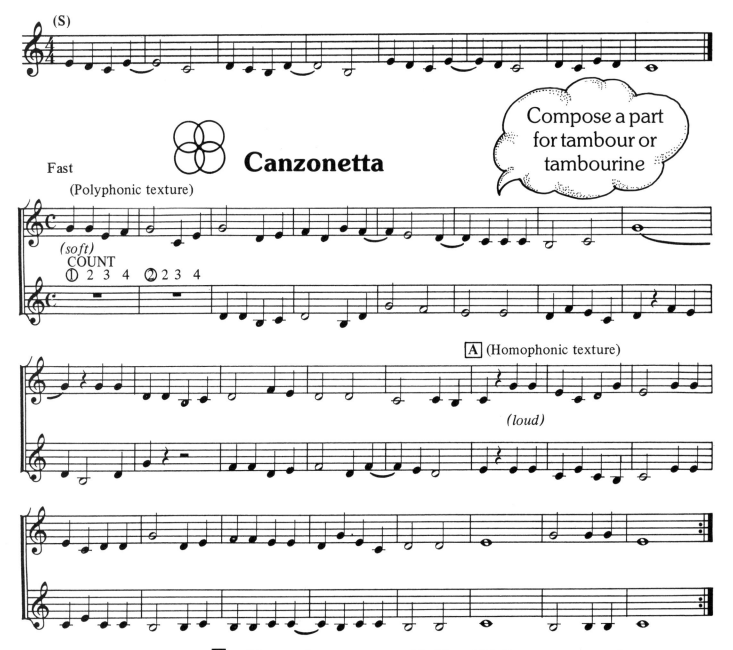

■ More tied notes on pages 18, 20 and 21. Preparatory rounds on pages 11 & 12.

Slurs (1)
and legato tonguing

	Valves
1	Open
2	2nd
3	1st
4	1st & 2nd
5	2nd & 3rd

Play all slurs on different valve combinations

Valve slur/legato tonguing

■ Proceed up to A; or to 'quavers' on page 22; or to F♯ on page 24; or to low A on page 36.

The note A

1st and
2nd valves

play these notes using varied rhythm patterns

F	A	D
A	C	E
D	A	D
E	G	G

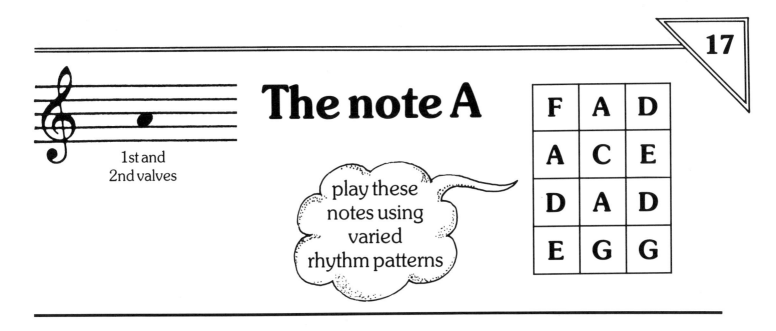

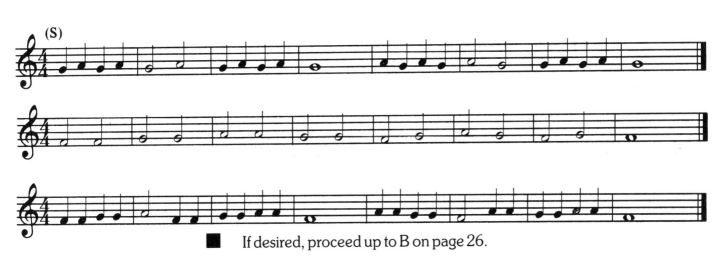

■ If desired, proceed up to B on page 26.

Pattern
(Based on the QUADRATONE)

Phrase A   Phrase B   Phrase A repeated   Phrase C
1   2   3   4

Slow round

play by ear

Continue   Continue

■ see *Accompaniments Book* concerning the QUADRATONE.

New rhythms

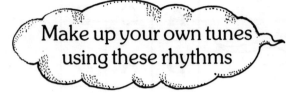

Make up your own tunes using these rhythms

(1)

(2)

(3)

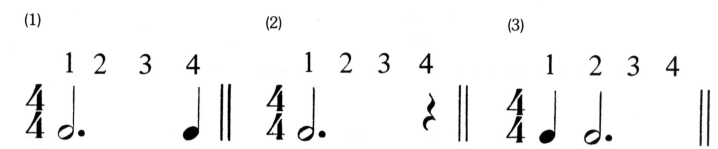

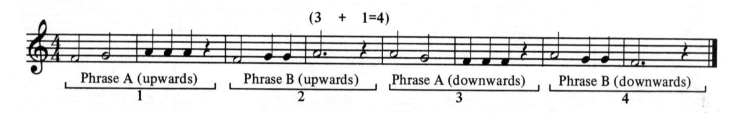

Stepping out

When the saints go marching in

■ Proceed to Low A, page 36; or up to B on page 26; or to B♭ on page 32; or to Quavers on page 22; or to F♯ on page 24. Related ensemble on pages 20 & 21.

Brass group warm-up 1

is the sign for PAUSE, meaning the note should be held beyond its normal value

Harmony long notes

(Optional 3rd part)

Practise tonguing on each note, devising your own rhythm patterns

Low G is played with 1st & 3rd valves

Unison long notes

Slurred slow notes

Slurred fast notes

Regal fanfare

Maestoso

¢ means TWO MINIM BEATS in each bar, ie $\frac{2}{2}$ time. (Sometimes called ALLA BREVE time)

*Fanfare part for timpani (or bass drum and tenor drum) and cymbals.

When used in conjunction with lower brass and horn, play fanfare twice through: (1) trumpets and timpani; (2) trumpets, lower brass, timpani and cymbals.

When I first came to this land

Traditional

Fast and furious

■ *When three trumpeters are sharing a lesson,* the third part for these ensemble pieces is to be found in the *Brass Band Book.*

On the repeat, omit these bars and go straight to the bar marked ⎾2⏌

Blowin' in the wind

Accompaniment for synthesizer on 'samba' rhythm setting

Play three times, then on to 'chorus'

4/4	B♭	E♭	F	B♭	B♭	E♭	F	F7

Chorus

E♭	F	B♭	Gmin	E♭	F	B♭	B♭

Quavers in 4/4 time

Quavers in 3/4 & 2/4 time

■ 2/4 Rhythm Grid on page 34.

Roundabout

This means 'rest' for 2 whole bars so count ①2, ②2 and then play from bar 3

Make up your own tune about something that moves quickly using quavers

Sleigh ride

Fast

loud

fairly loud

very loud

The note F sharp

Key-signature

key signature for G Major

A SHARP placed thus, at the beginning of the line, means all F's are sharpened

Slavic slurs

Smoothly

■ To be played with *legato tonguing* or *slurring* throughout, as directed.

F sharps & quavers

Austrian Holiday

F/F♯ Study

Lilting

(Accent)

Fine   *slower*

D.C. al Fine
a tempo

■ Related ensemble on page 37.

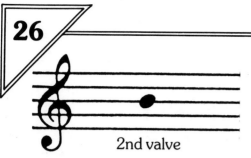

2nd valve

The note B

Sing hosanna

Merrily

Traditional

Victorian ballad

In relaxed style

Fine

D.C. al Fine

This stands for DA CAPO AL FINE, which means go back to the beginning and end at the bar marked FINE

■ B flat (page 32) can be introduced before B, if desired.

Workin' on the railroad

Like a jolly cowboy saloon song

Traditional

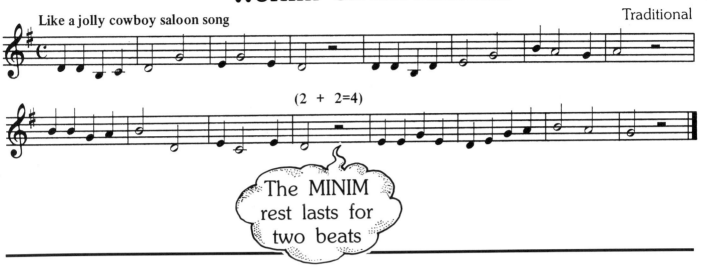

(2 + 2=4)

> The MINIM rest lasts for two beats

5/4 time

(1 2 3 4 5)
(S)

> In 5/4 every bar adds up to five crotchet beats.

Waiting!

(S)

Play by ear

Continue   Continue

Relevant ensemble: B with quavers, page 37.

Upper C

open

Scale and arpeggio of C

C chromatic scale

Intervals

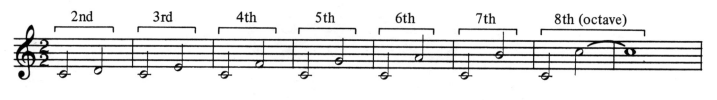

Look for scale patterns

Round the scale

You will find a GLOSSARY of musical terms on page 62

Study in C

play by ear

Try playing by ear, your favourites from the world of classics, pop or TV.

	Valves
1	Open
2	2nd
3	1st
4	1st & 2nd
5	2nd & 3rd
6	1st & 3rd
7	1st, 2nd & 3rd

Slurs (2)
And valve slurs/legato tonguing

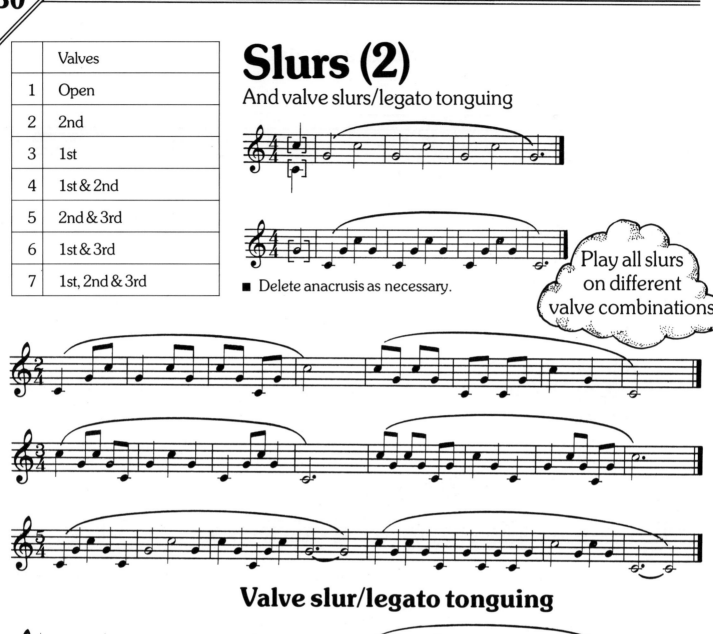

■ Delete anacrusis as necessary.

> Play all slurs on different valve combinations

Valve slur/legato tonguing

* Upper D on page 35

> The FLAT lowers the pitch of a note by one semitone (see page 32)

Relaxation

Plainchant

Play 'freely', i.e. not with a strict pulse

Laus — de - o pat - ri, pa - ri - li que —

pro - li, et ti - bi sanc - te stu - di - o pe - ren - ni spi - ri - tus

nos - tro — re - so - net a - bo — - - re

om — - - ne per — - - ae - vum.

Refer to the CHROMATIC SCALE (page 28) for
any notes you don't already know

My favourite things

From *The Sound of Music*

Words by OSCAR HAMMERSTEIN II
Music by RICHARD RODGERS

Allegro

mp

mf

1,2

2

3

f

f

mp crescendo

f

2

Chromatic scale on page 28. Proceed up to D, page 35; or down to A, page 36; or to B♭, page 32; or to quavers, page 34.

The note B flat

1st valve

The FLAT lowers the pitch of a note by one semitone

F	G	A	B♭	E	A	F
C	B♭	D	G	F	C	E

D minor round

We wish you a Merry Christmas
Traditional

Fast and jolly

play by ear

Continue

Continue

■ Related ensemble, page 49; F scale, page 52; D minor scale, pages 58 & 59.

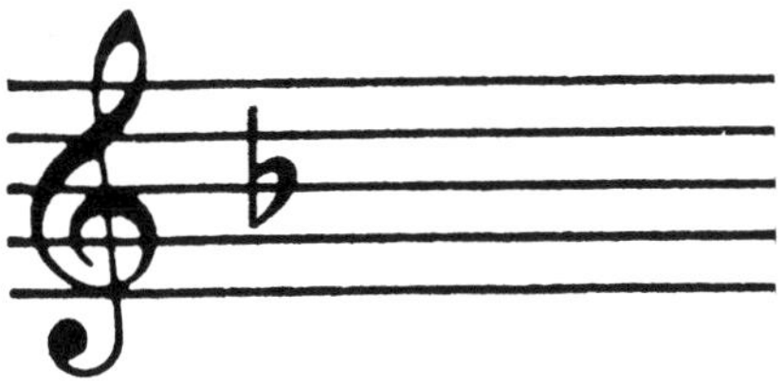

Key-signature of F major / D minor

Yankee Doodle

Traditional

B♭
1

Aura Lee

Traditional

The natural sign

2nd valve

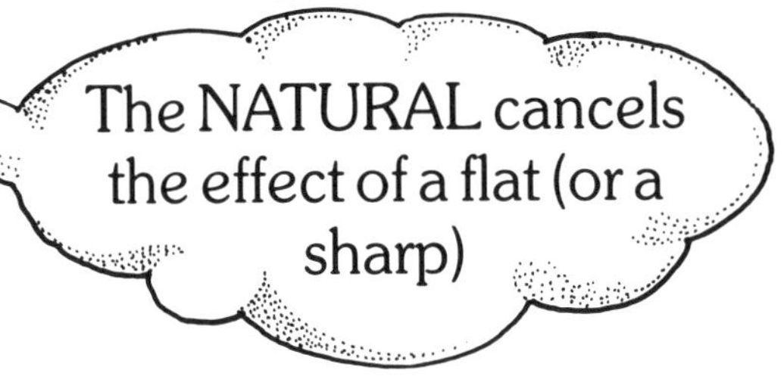
The NATURAL cancels the effect of a flat (or a sharp)

F major round

(1)
(S)
(2)

Coventry carol

Traditional

(♭)
*

*Upper D on page 35.

Quavers up to C

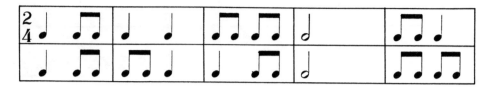

Quaver study

Allegro

■ Syncopated quavers on page 44; semiquavers on page 40; dotted crotchet on page 42; $\frac{6}{8}$ quavers on page 41; dotted quavers on page 50.

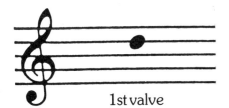

1st valve

Upper D

Limp round

(1)   (2)   (3)

Edelweiss
From *The Sound of Music*

words by OSCAR HAMMERSTEIN II
music by RICHARD RODGERS

Semplice

mp

f

rall.....................................

Continue   Continue

■ $\frac{6}{8}$ up to D, page 39; quavers up to D, pages 39, 45; semiquavers up to D, page 40. D major key on page 47. Relaxation exercises on page 30. Dotted-crotchet/quaver, page 42.

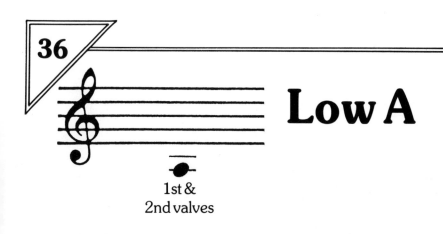

Low A

1st &
2nd valves

Quadratone pattern

Compose your own
piece using the notes of
the QUADRATONE*

Low round

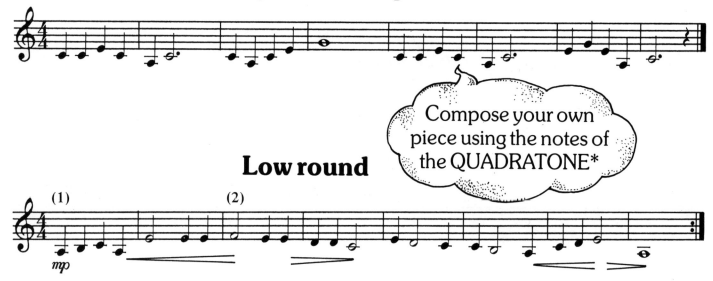

mp

Theme from Polovtsian dances

ALEXANDER BORODIN (1833-87)

Lilting, not fast

mp (mf)

■ Related ensemble on pages 37 and 48.
*A useful group of notes requiring open and 1/2 fingering only.

Au claire de la lune

Traditional

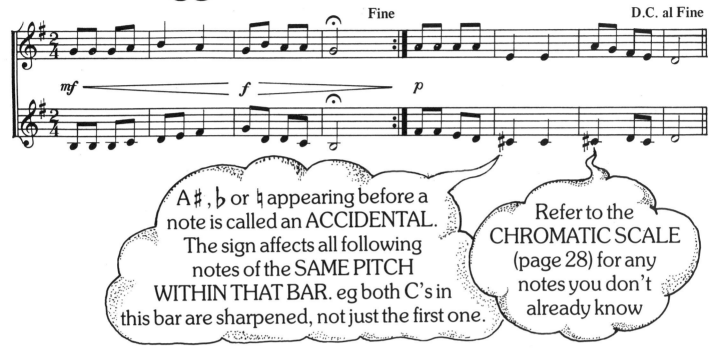

A♯, ♭ or ♮ appearing before a note is called an ACCIDENTAL. The sign affects all following notes of the SAME PITCH WITHIN THAT BAR. eg both C's in this bar are sharpened, not just the first one.

Refer to the CHROMATIC SCALE (page 28) for any notes you don't already know

Little donkey

words and music by ERIC BOSWELL

Preparatory C♯ exercises on page 47.

Brass group warm-up 2

Harmony long notes

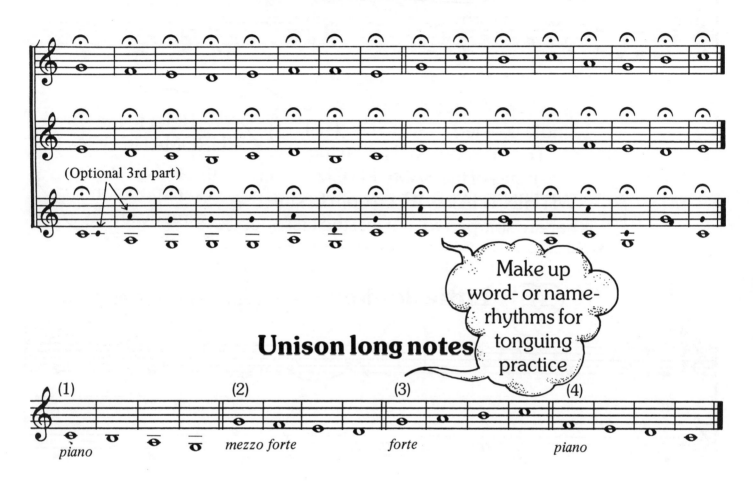

(Optional 3rd part)

Make up word- or name-rhythms for tonguing practice

Unison long notes

(1) piano   (2) mezzo forte   (3) forte   (4) piano

Scale exercise

(S) piano   crescendo   forte   diminuendo   piano   p ——— f ——— p ——— f

Slurs

(1)

(2)

■ more level (2) slurs on page 30.

Tijuana brass

I saw three ships

Traditional

Semiquavers in 2/4

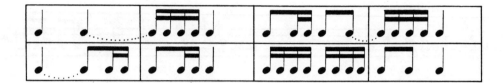

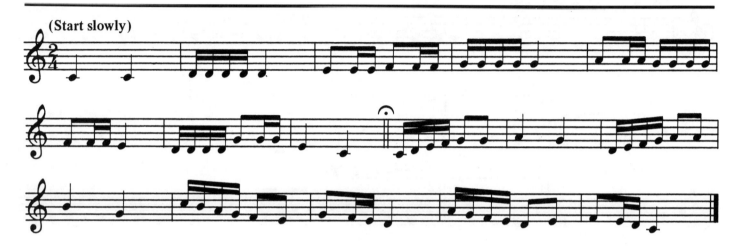

(Start slowly)

Semiquaver study

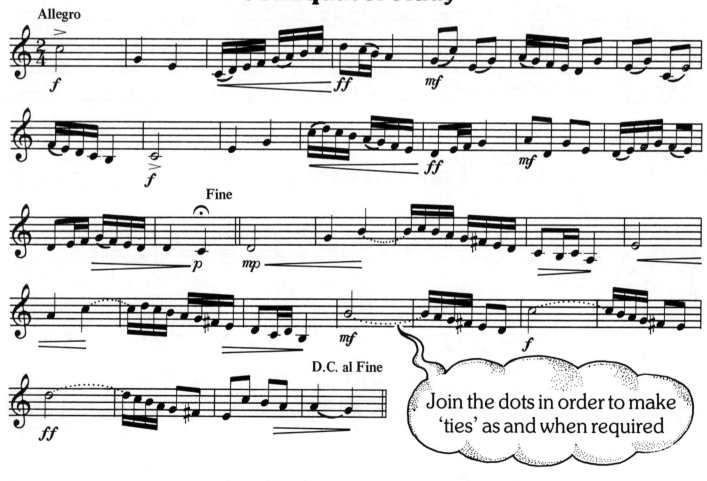

Join the dots in order to make 'ties' as and when required

Related ensemble on pages 48 and 55.

Related ensemble on page 39.

The dotted crotchet in $\frac{4}{4}$

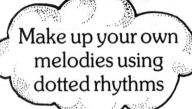

Make up your own melodies using dotted rhythms

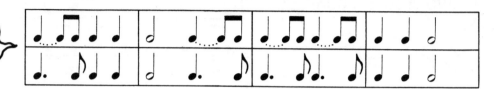

Join the dots to make the dotted-crotchet/quaver effect

Theme
from *"New World"* Symphony

ANTONIN DVOŘÁK
(1841-1904)

Quick march

Composed by nine-year old
REBECKA ELEY

'Ode to joy'

LUDWIG VAN BEETHOVEN
(1770-1827)

Allegro assai

Play by ear

Continue

Continue

■ Related ensemble on pages 48 and 49.

The dotted crotchet in $\frac{3}{4}$ and $\frac{2}{4}$

Compose your own piece about an interesting place or far-away country

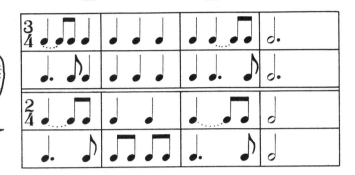

Scottish ballad

Legato e cantabile

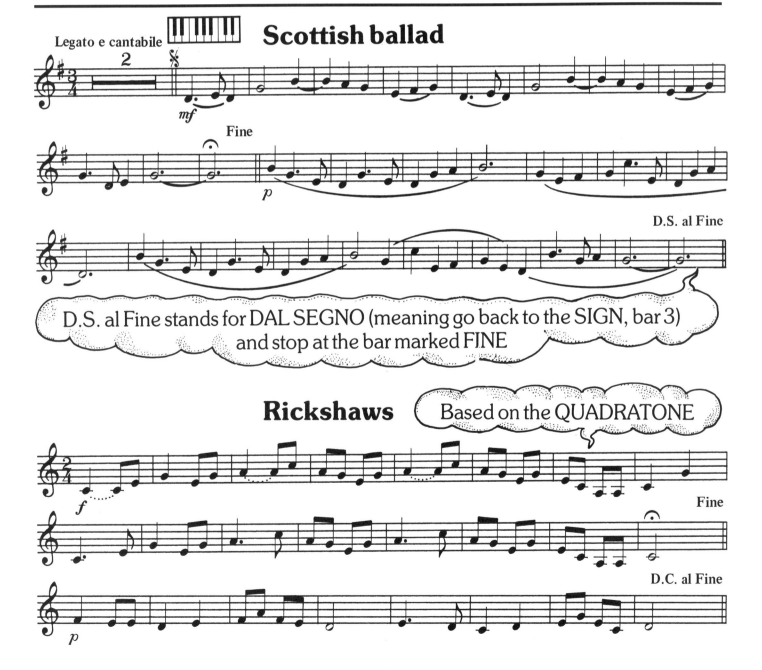

D.S. al Fine stands for DAL SEGNO (meaning go back to the SIGN, bar 3) and stop at the bar marked FINE

Rickshaws — Based on the QUADRATONE

See *Accompaniments Book* concerning the QUADRATONE.

Quaver syncopation

To be played (A) in strict time
and (B) in swinging time

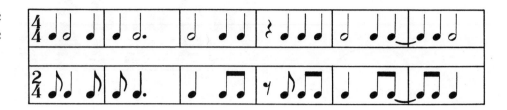

Old Liza Jane

See Glossary for new signs

Caribbean dance

Traditional

Tempo di Rumba

Fine

D.C. al Fine

play by ear

Continue

■ Syncopated crotchets on pages 12, 15 and 21; Related ensemble on page 39. * Upper E on page 50.

Simply blue
Twelve bar blues

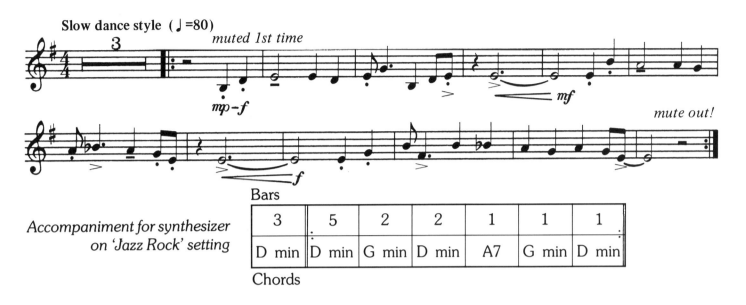

Accompaniment for synthesizer on 'Jazz Rock' setting

Bars

3	5	2	2	1	1	1
D min	D min	G min	D min	A7	G min	D min

Chords

West Indian carnival

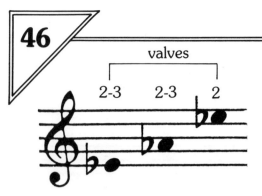

valves

2-3   2-3   2

The notes A flat and E flat

Key-signature of E♭ major

Villikins and his Dinah

Traditional

mp   *mf*

f   *mf*   *p*

The swinger

Twelve bar blues

Swinging style (♩ =132)

f

Pattern 1   Pattern 2

f

ff   Pattern 3   *mf*

Suggested variation

(ossia)

mf   *f*

ff   *mp*   *ff*

Accompaniment for synthesizer on '16 beat' rhythm setting

Bars					
4	2	2	1	1	2
E♭ min	A♭ min	E♭ min	B♭ 7	A♭ min	E♭ min

Chords   (B♭7 ♭13)

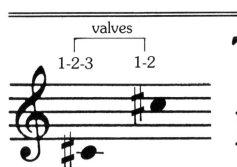

valves
1-2-3   1-2

The note C sharp
Key-signature of D major

Canon

THOMAS TALLIS (c. 1505-1585)

(1)   (2)   (3)   (4)

Lasst uns erfreuen
Chorale Melody

rit.................... a tempo

mf   mf   f   mf

mp   p <   <   mf <   <   f

L.A. Nitespot

Slow swing style (♩=c.100)
muted 1st time

Twelve bar blues

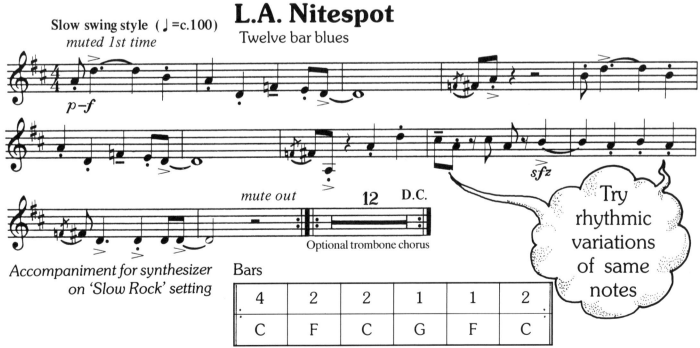

p-f

sfz

Try rhythmic variations of same notes

mute out   **12**   D.C.

Optional trombone chorus

Accompaniment for synthesizer on 'Slow Rock' setting

Bars

4	2	2	1	1	2
C	F	C	G	F	C

■ Scale of D minor on page 58.

Chords

Michael row the boat

Traditional

Canzona

ADRIANO BANCHIERI (1568-1634)

(Part 1)

(Part 2)

Compose an accompaniment for Tambour using crotchets, quavers and semi-quavers

■ Because the CANZONA is a four-part polyphonic piece, the parts above cannot be played simply as a trumpet duet. Third and fourth parts are to be found in all other *Team Brass* books.

O Little Town of Bethlehem Traditional

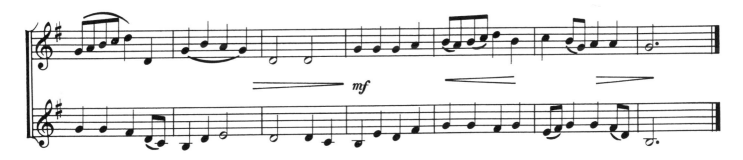

St. Anthony chorale JOSEPH HAYDN (1732-1809)

Upper E

open

I gave my love a cherry

Traditional

Andante cantabile

mp   *mf*   *mf*

pp

The dotted quaver

Theme

Canon

Gustav Mahler (1860-1911)

Langsam

(1)   (2)

pp

(3)   (4)

■ 'Relaxation' exercises on page 30.

Say 'goodbye'
From the opera *Marriage of Figaro*

WOLFGANG AMADEUS MOZART (1756-1791)

Triplet quaver group - Three quavers played in the time of one crotchet

Old Spanish town

play by ear

Extra material up to E on pages 44, 48, 49, 54, 58 and 59.

Upper F

1st valve

Scale & arpeggio of F

The first noel

Traditional

The centipede's masterpiece

composed by fifteen-year old SARAH HART

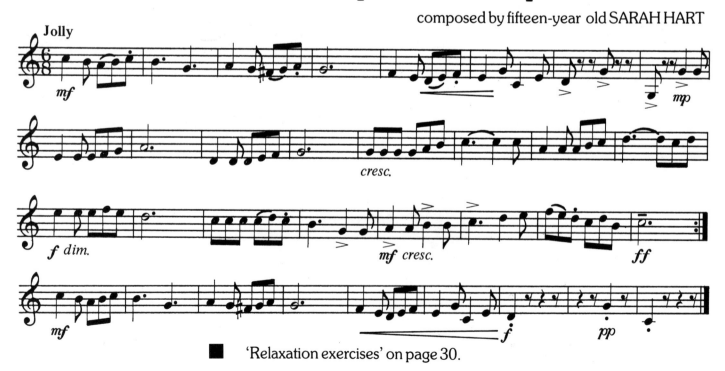

■ 'Relaxation exercises' on page 30.

Pomp and circumstance

EDWARD ELGAR (1857-1934)

Gallop

from the opera *Orpheus in the Underworld*

JACQUES OFFENBACH (1819-1880)

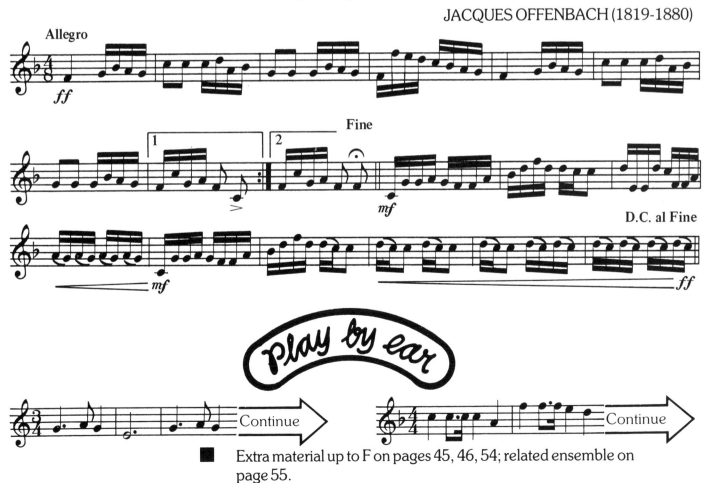

■ Extra material up to F on pages 45, 46, 54; related ensemble on page 55.

Slurs (3)

Intervals

(slurred and tongued)

Chromatic scale

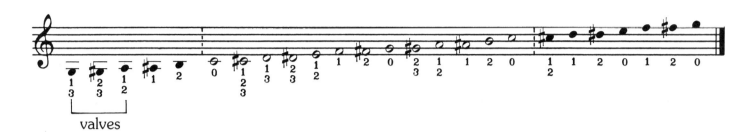

valves

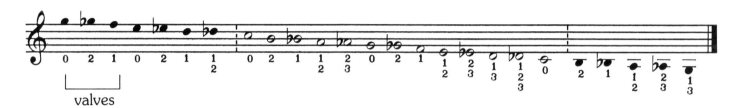

valves

 # March

from *Judas Maccabaeus*

GEORGE FRIDERIC HANDEL (1685-1759)

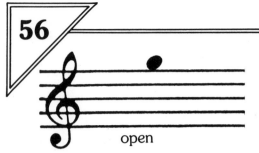

Upper G

open

(1)   (2)   (3)   (4)

Chorale

HANS HASSLER (1564-1612)

Legato e cantabile

mp   *mf*   *p*

'Star Wars' Main Title

JOHN WILLIAMS

Allegro assai

f   *3*   *3*   *3*   *3*

To Coda ⊕

f   *3*   *3*   *3*   *mf*

D.𝄋 al Coda

f   *3*   *ff*

⊕ CODA

ff   *fff*

D.S. al Coda means repeat the section from 𝄋 to ⊕ and then cut to the CODA section

'Relaxation exercises' on page 30.

Scale of G major

March

from *Occasional Oratorio*

GEORGE FRIDERIC HANDEL (1685-1759)

'Running' scale of G

■ Extra material up to G on pages 56, 60 and 61.

Scales and arpeggios

A minor harmonic

A minor melodic

Arpeggio of A minor

D minor harmonic

■ D major on page 47 ### D minor melodic

E major

■ E flat major, page 46

E minor harmonic

E minor melodic

C major

Arpeggio of C major

B♭ major

Arpeggio of B♭ major

Slurs (4)

'Relaxation exercises' on page 30.

Grand finale

Printed by Halstan & Co. Ltd., Amersham, Bucks., England

Glossary of musical terms

MUSICAL TERM	ABBREVIATION	MEANING IN ENGLISH
forte	*f*	loudly
mezzoforte	*mf*	(lit. half) moderately loud
piano	*p*	softly
mezzopiano	*mp*	(lit. half) moderately softly
fortissimo	*ff*	very loudly
pianissimo	*pp*	very softly
crescendo	*cresc.* or ◁	getting louder
diminuendo	*dim.* or ▷	getting quieter
ritenuto/ritardando	*rit.*	getting slower
a tempo		at the original speed
tempo		speed
subito	*sub.*	suddenly
Moderato		at a moderate speed
Allegro		merry, quick, bright
Grandioso		grandly
Con brio		with spirit
simile	*sim.*	Continue playing in same style
Langsam		slowly
Da Capo (Al fine)	D.C. or D.C. al Fine	Go back to the beginning (and stop at the place marked Fine)
Presto		quickly
staccato	♩ ♩ ♩	detached, ie, the opposite of Legato
tenuto	♩ ♩ ♩	Hold for full value
rallentando	*rall.*	gradually slowing down
Religioso		religiously
Semplice		simply
Andante		at walking pace
Maestoso		majestically
Adagio		slowly
piano-(forte)	*p(f)*	Play quietly first time, and loudly when music is repeated
Common time	**C**	$\frac{4}{4}$ ie four crotchets per bar
Alla Breve	**¢**	$\frac{2}{2}$ ie two minim beats per bar
Dal Segno	D. 𝄋 (al Coda)	Go back to the 'sign' (and then go to Coda')
Assai		very
Legato		smoothly
Cantabile		in a singing style
Et / E }		and
Ossia		alternative